REDEMPTION OF THE SHATTERED: A TEENAGER'S HEALING JOURNEY THROUGH SANDTRAY THERAPY

REDEMPTION OF THE SHATTERED: A TEENAGER'S HEALING JOURNEY THROUGH SANDTRAY THERAPY

By

Bob Livingstone LCSW

REDEMPTION OF THE SHATTERED: A TEENAGER'S HEALING JOURNEY THROUGH SANDTRAY THERAPY

MORE ADVANCE PRAISE FOR *REDEMPTION OF THE SHATTERED: A TEENAGER'S HEALING JOURNEY THROUGH SANDTRAY THERAPY*

"The narrative in this book is alive. The story is so vivid and compelling that it reaches out and draws you in, leaving you standing next to Rob at his father's funeral, or meeting the demons with him and cringing from the witches and monsters. While I have certainly read many books about grief, death and the healing process, I found myself riveted by Rob and his experiences.

This is a clear and coherent description of the experience of being shattered by the death of a parent, and of working through a trauma, from denial to resolution and redemption. What is unique about this book, however, is the power of the story in the sandtray. It unfolds like a novel I could not put down.

As I was inexorably drawn into the emotional world of the tray and of this teenage boy, and felt the turmoil, guilt, despair and numbing right along with him, I was given the opportunity to experience Rob's world with great immediacy. I went with him through the transformation of his inner demons into the protective allies they always were, and to a deepening experience of reliving old trauma, revisiting it again and again until it was resolved, and then of his finding the gem in the darkness of his past experiences. The story was also a wonderful metaphor for the experience of therapy, the possibility of transformation and the release of energy, previously stuck and inflicted on the self, into creativity and healing.

Bob's intelligent commentary adds a deeper layer to the story and draws together the loose ends. His family questions should be a real stimulus to authentic conversation between parents and children.

Ultimately, in Bob's willingness to disclose and offer us the gift of his suffering, to lay it open for us to witness and experience with him in the tray, he has done us all a very great service, and shown others how it is possible to heal one's heart and open up to life and to spirituality, to love and to forgiveness."

Kathy Carlson PhD MFT

"As the mother of two teenage girls, I found this book especially insightful because it is not the usual litanies regarding what teenagers experience or how to cope with their feelings. This book embodies the actual thoughts and feelings of a real teenager. It is never 'sugarcoated'. A boy or girl can identify with Rob because he is 'cool'; he's hanging out, doing drugs, cigarettes dangling from his lips. A teenager would think, 'hey, that could be me.'"

Ann Blumstein mother of two teenage daughters

"In *Redemption of the Shattered*, Bob Livingstone has created a collection of visual images and descriptions that will inevitably help teenagers and adults open up their grieving process. He gives countless examples of his experiences, which serve as a guide for people who are unsure how to give a voice to what they feel about the death of a loved one. I recommend reading the commentary and family discussion for each chapter as a means to using this book as a tool towards healing. *Redemption of the Shattered* would also be useful as a supplemental text to a class on the process of sandtray."

Moby Coquillard MA. Licensed Marriage and Family Therapist

"Bob Livingstone has clearly articulated a multitude of emotional experiences relating to the death of his father. These experiences are not often addressed in popular culture and media. He manages to address feelings of grief, pain, confusion and joy in a unique way. *Redemption of the Shattered* illustrates that Sandtray Therapy is a powerful vehicle for deep discovery, understanding and healing."

Toni DeMarco Marriage and Family Therapist

"I highly recommend *Redemption of the Shattered* for anyone searching for psychological and spiritual insight. The book also includes helpful guidelines for dealing with grief and/or the painful alienation between teens and parents."

Sharon Kman, M.S., Certified Rehabilitation Counselor and Marriage and Family Therapist with 20 years experience working with teens and their families.

TABLE OF CONTENTS

DEDICATIONS

To the memories of Othello, Nikki, Lavya, and Joe. They all left us much too soon.

EDITOR'S NOTE

Redemption of the Shattered is a brave, challenging and uniquely rewarding work. Think of it as a video game where, instead of sitting safely in your room pushing buttons or pulling on a joystick, you're inside with the monsters, fighting for your life. The monsters may come from your own mind, but that doesn't make them any less real. They may attack with guilt, fear and shame, instead of with guns or blades, but they are deadly just the same.

Like a video game, *Redemption of the Shattered* plays out on different levels. To survive each level, Rob needs to learn new skills, find new help, and discover new strengths. Each of the 24 levels brings a new treasure, too. But, as in a video game, successfully completing one level brings Rob face-to-face with old and new demons on the next level.

Having to face the same trials over and over, when you think you've beaten them, is one of the few similarities between video games and life. It would be nice if our inner demons stayed dead, but they usually don't. They have to be faced, accepted and transformed repeatedly, over time.

Redemption shows us how to follow that long, spiraling, often frustrating path. It is not a self-help book, though, and it is not easy. It is an adventure through time, space, mind and spirit. Rob moves from teenage to adulthood and back, and is sometimes in both places at once. A large number of characters come and go, and the author leaves it to us to understand their significance.

As much as possible, I have tried to preserve Bob Livingstone's highly original voice. The story requires us to remain flexible about time and person, and to a certain extent about grammar. It's worth the effort, though. *Redemption* will challenge you, but will also reward you with scenes of great beauty, a message of profound hope, and a new understanding of grief and what it takes to over come it. I hope and believe you will gain as much from reading it as I did from editing it.

-- David Spero, RN. Author of *The Art of Getting Well: a Five-step Plan for Maximizing Health When You Have a Chronic Illness* (Hunter House, 2002) E-mail david@DavidSperoRN.com

INTRODUCTION
November 1, 2001

Without warning, death has been thrust upon fifteen-year-old Bob Livingstone. His worldview collapses as he is catapulted into a tumultuous journey of finding himself and meaning in life. Twenty-five years later, successful in the eyes of the world, Bob shows up in my Sandtray-Worldplay Studio, finally ready to face that day and the shattered terrain of his inner psycho-spiritual landscape. Using dramatic play with images in a tray of sand, he repeatedly journeys deep into this inner landscape to make sense of his experiences.

He faces the demons and the saints, callous abuse and tender love, guilt and forgiveness, abandonment and guidance. He gradually learns to face the coffin, the grave, the Mother and Sister, Father and the pantheon of gods within. As he heals himself through fully experiencing his dramatic play in the sandtray, he begins to understand the cycle of birth and death. He retrieves his Soul and his heartfulness. He can respond to the preciousness of life. He begins to lovingly embrace himself, others and humanity.

Redemption of the Shattered is an exciting resource for adolescents, parents, educators, psychotherapists and those who work with the challenges of adolescence. It is a frank, down to earth teaching for those who are faced with difficult and abusive circumstances, those who are grieving and who are 'plagued' by the cyclic revisiting of hurts, pains, and by the misunderstandings engendered by false belief systems. It neither simplifies nor glorifies the struggle of finding life's meaning. It shows how difficult the task of sorting out the chaos of our secret, inner world can be when we do not or cannot access the healing power of images and play, or the supportive sharing with family, friends and community.

Redemption of the Shattered offers parents a graphic insight into the misbehavior and lostness of their adolescents who were once babies that were loved ever so dearly. Adolescents are given rich insight into the intense self-absorption that frequently plagues their wounded parents, who struggle so hard to survive emotionally and economically, and who all too often compensate for their frustrating failures by turning against their own children with physical and emotional violence. Educators and therapists may use this book to guide and support students and clients who have faced such loss and are learning how to grieve.

Bob Livingstone vividly describes the long spiral path towards healing the guilt, shame, abuse, terror, and estrangement that he encounters during his Sandtray-Worldplay journey. This allows any reader to develop patience with themselves or with significant others that are engaged in an integrative healing process. *Redemption of the Shattered* encourages everyone to make use of the rich power of images and their own inner wisdom for healing old and new wounds, and for bringing understanding between members of families and communities.

Families, teachers and students are invited to discuss the down-to-earth and undisguised discussion questions that are offered in *Redemption of the Shattered*. These are sure to open the doors to the inner world, and allow families and communities to overcome existing taboos against acknowledging, experiencing and responding to traumatic life-changing events. Whether people face their sadness and loss, their guilt and rage, or the joy and love that emerge on the difficult journey, intimacy, forgiveness, compassion and the ability to be in the present are surely possible.

Gisela Schubach DeDomenico Ph. D
Oakland, California
510-530-1383
gisela@dnai.com

PREFACE

Teenage Trauma – such as divorce, substance abuse, violence or loss of a loved one – creates internal demons that can lead to self-destruction. Sandtray Therapy can connect teens to an inner world of which they may have no awareness. Once the inner world is discovered, teens have the opportunity to take a difficult but rewarding journey, where they can define, face and transform these internal demons.

Fifteen-year old Rob, the story's protagonist, begins his journey at his father's funeral. He soon meets the Wicked Witch, an internal demon whose job is to instill guilt and self-hatred. As the story unfolds, Rob learns that pushing her away and denying her existence creates increased turmoil. He discovers ways to face her directly. He eventually learns that she was originally constructed to protect him from the pain of his father's death, and she becomes an ally instead on an enemy.

This scenario of breaking through the denial, facing the internal demons and beginning the transformational process is a theme that flows throughout the book. This scenario is known as integration. This is an avenue that teens can follow in order to heal the wounds from trauma.

This book provides parents and teens a way to face "stuck" loss and pain by breaking through fear. It informs readers how they can transform this state of "stuckness" to the opening of the heart and discovery of forgiveness. It teaches how to resolve trauma by demonstrating how the author worked through his anguish.

This is a story of a fifteen-year-old boy who starts out feeling lost, isolated, afraid and guilt-ridden. He feels that he has no one to talk to and has great difficulty in expressing his true feelings. This story is based on the true-life experiences of the author.

Rob's healing journey occurs in the world of Sandtray Therapy, a world of powerful, vital images. Allow me to describe the Sandtray therapist's office. It is an inviting, stimulating and creative setting. There are several small sandtrays held above the ground on stands. These sandtrays are approximately 20 inches by 30 inches and 3 to 4 inches deep. White, green, black, and purple sand fills each tray. There are rows and rows of shelves with hundreds of miniature figures. Farm animals, religious icons, cartoon characters, trees, stones, regular people, super heroes and heroines, monsters and angels are some of the figures on display. Pitchers of water are available to pour into the trays.

The client is encouraged to choose figures from the shelves that move her in some manner and place them in the tray. The therapist then asks the client about the sandtray world she has created.

In Sandtray Therapy, the client is encouraged to be exactly where they are, and they are allowed to play with their situation by placing figures in the sandtray. The sandtray process teaches you that it is ok to be who you are, and if you play with it, by moving and changing figures in the sand, your life can transform.

Personal trauma is a theme that is frequently created in the tray. Those traumas may be child abuse, divorce, disasters, or death of a loved one. Memories, feelings, understandings, and experiences are continually created in the sand. They can then be faced and worked through on an intellectual, emotional and spiritual level.

The "working through" was an important aspect of the Sandtray Therapy I experienced. The figures and corresponding scenes were alive and visible. The placing of the figures and their connection with other figures in the tray touched me deep inside.

I learned that Sandtray Therapy could deal with trauma and loss in a way that regular talk therapy often does not reach. The figures are placed directly in front of the builder. The painful memories and feelings emerge during scenes in the tray. The builder is able to hold these painful scenes because they are standing in front of him. This is different from regular talk therapy where the memories reside only in one's head. In talk therapy, the memories are discussed and intellectualized, but not seen or experienced.

Regular talk therapy tends to give much of the power in the session to the therapist. She asks leading questions designed to break through defenses and the resistance of the client, in order to help him gain insight about his problems. During Sandtray Therapy sessions, the client is more active and in control. She is building her own scene, working on her own issues. Instead of having the primary relationship between the therapist and the client, with work proceeding through transference (perceptions of significant people in the client's life that are transferred to the therapist), the primary focus is between the client and the sandtray. The Sandtray therapist serves as a guide and a container of a safe space.

The Sandtray therapist attempts to assist the client in accepting her own healing powers to heal the psyche, Although healing and transformation do occur in talk therapy, the talk therapist tends to attempt to be the main healing object during the sessions, where the client may become dependent on the interaction with the therapist and may not focus on the healing process within.

Gisela Schubach De Domenico Ph.D. is a nationally recognized expert on Sandtray Therapy. She has been my teacher since 1991. One of her teachings that I have incorporated in my work is that one's psyche works through issues related to the personal, then moves to the family, then the societal, and on to ancestors, to humanity as a whole, to the transpersonal to the universal.

Rob's (my) healing process follows the spiral path Dr. De Domenico describes. It moves from personal isolation to deep connection. The first scene I created was *Funeral Day*. I assembled my father's casket, the Rabbi, my mother and sister together. I did not know what the purpose of this creation was until I talked about the scene. I realized that I was not really present for his funeral, that I had really never experienced the full impact of that day.

The sandtray work solidified my belief as a therapist that in order to heal from past trauma, one needs to work through it by returning to the memory and original action of that trauma. I also learned that there is no limit to the times one can benefit from returning to the trauma. As you will see, I created many scenes that took place at my father's grave. I returned to the grave and demons many times. Returning is a natural part of grieving. Along the way, I experienced many moments of insight and consolation.

But healing rarely occurs in a single flash, no matter how powerful and enlightening the experience may be. Like Rob, I often experienced relief and release in the sandtray world, only to find that the demons and fears were still there in full force. Returning is a natural part of working through trauma. This is a teaching that seems to be left out of most self-help/how to books. The beginning sessions were painful, but I eventually found a way to return to the grave without the heaviness and numbness. My repeat visits to the grave brought growing wisdom.

Writing this book has educated me in how to assist my own clients who have experienced a loss or have been victimized by abuse. Each chapter represents one or more sandtray sessions. The action, although alternating between present and past, is described in present tense. The reader is taken directly into the graveyard, hospital or bedroom.

Each chapter includes a chapter heading with black and white photos of the sandtrays, a narrative section, which tells the story, and a commentary section that discusses the Sandtray Therapy process, the major figures utilized, and the teachings learned from the chapter. The reader has the option of reading the entire book in the sequence it was created, or going through the narrative sections in turn, following Rob's journey, and returning to the commentary when desired.

A family discussion section follows each commentary, with questions designed to inspire family members to discuss how this particular chapter affected them. It is my hope that these questions will lead to improved communication and healing between teenagers and their parents. This book allows for the lifting of taboos around traumatic issues. It provides parents with language and images they can use to communicate with their children about such difficult issues.

This is not a traditional self-help book with a definitive step-by-step process you explicitly follow in order to reach salvation. Instead, you are asked to travel with Rob as he makes his journey, meeting the Demons, The Voice of Wisdom, Gods and Goddesses and eventually his father. You are invited to step into Rob's shoes as he breaks through the denial of death and the denial of the goodness of life. It is hoped that you can connect with Rob's struggle, courage and transformation. It is also hoped that this healing journey inspires you to seek out Sandtray Therapy.

CHAPTER ONE

FUNERAL DAY

CHAPTER ONE

FUNERAL DAY

Rob recklessly smacks his hand through the first floor apartment window. He is lucky that no arteries are severed or blood splattered. He is angry, no, enraged. He has no idea why he is so upset. Every day that passes is experienced as prolonged agony. He has reached the fourth decade of his life and happiness continues to elude him. He has no sense of security and worries all the time. He wonders what the pain in his stomach is about. He pushes away all those he loves by intimidation and sheer cruelty. Isolation and alienation follow him everywhere. Life has become a cruel mystery. The intense turmoil always leads back to a profound agitated despondency.

This nearly middle-aged man does have the sense that his problems began a long time ago. He does not want to investigate his past, although a force inside pushes him back…way, way back………..

Rob finds himself in a dark cave, a place he goes to escape the pressures of acting normal in front of others. The gangly teenager lights his first Marlboro of the day as he paces the cave's floor. The smoke is taken deep into his lungs and then released into the dankness. The smoke swirls around the cave as the radio plays mid-1960's rock and roll in the background. The hypnotic effect of the music's rhythm combined with the haze in the cave cause Rob to get up and walk further into the cavern. The smoke has become so thick he can barely breathe. He is choking and only has enough energy to find his way to daylight. He tumbles out of the cave and falls onto the ground.

His eyes sting from the smoke and he has difficulty seeing. Eventually the blurring clears and he becomes acquainted with the surroundings. Look, over there! He sees a long street with two-story houses constructed right next to each other. They are painted a variety of drab colors, obviously not an architect's dream. Oh, there is his white house on the corner with the screened-in back porch. There is his father in gray chinos and an old flannel shirt walking to the family car, the putrid brown Mercury Comet. A billed cap hides his face. The car sputters to life and pulls away from the curve.

Rob watches the Comet as it reaches the highway. Suddenly it begins swerving and crossing lanes as the honking of horns interrupts suburban routine. The brown car barely misses a head -on collision. A police car's siren comes screaming up behind Rob's father and demands that he pulls over. The police officer rushes out of his car and immediately inspects the driver's side of the Comet. Rob's father is gasping for breath and his face is blue as he falls into a coma.

An ambulance rushes him off to the hospital. Rob runs towards his house and his grandfather greets him with a somber look of anguish. "You're father died of a stroke today. He was fifty-six years old."

Rob quickly returns to the cave and attempts to push away all that he has just experienced. Although the cave is very warm, he is freezing and his hands tremble as he turns up the volume on the radio. The song bursts out in a soulful dirge like Motown's greatest hits jamming all at once "My heart is broken, no tears have spoken, what really matters when your whole life is shattered?" He believes that the song should resonate with him, but he is unsure of what he thinks, feels or needs.   The distant voice of his mother echoes in the cave. He cannot make out her sad words and the next moment he is with his mother and sister inside a limousine.

He looks out the window and sees the barren suburban wasteland that New Jersey becomes in winter. The trees are lifeless and the grass is brown or turned into frozen mud. He looks at his legs, arms and fingers. He realizes this is his body, but today every moment is projected as some hideous movie, someone else's film that moves slowly and without pace. He fears that this movie is endless. Rob feels alienated from all life forms. He does not know who he is, where he is going or why he has to go there.

The limo stops in front of a temple and his family gets out and walks inside. Rob notices the man in the front, the leader of this service, the Rabbi. He has a bald head and is muscular. He wears a purple shirt and pants. He is strong and self-assured. Maybe he can tell Rob what is going on.

Rob sits down amongst his family and friends, but he does not feel that he is actually in the room. He wonders if he is on some other planet observing the ritual of a funeral service conducted on earth.

23

The Rabbi asks Rob to visit with him in private for a couple of minutes. The Rabbi's bald head glistens with sweat and witch hazel. He says, "I don't know you, I don't know your mother, sister or your father. Why are you here?" The sinister Rabbi displays his impatience with Rob's non-answer with a dismissive wave of his multi-ringed hand.

The Rabbi begins the service by saying, "The deceased did not have a Jewish name, and although I did not know him at all, I am certain that he was a decent sort." The Rabbi sneaks a look a Rob and smirks. He continues, "His son had some idea that I am supposed to be of great assistance today, that I am supposed to ease the pain and explain what death is, but he is just a young fool. He hasn't yet learned that I am doing this for show and for my cut of the funeral action."

Rob is stunned and is unsure if he should beat the Rabbi senseless with his fists or throw up. He decides to go outside and puke, but a woman who looks remarkably like a witch intercepts him. She has moldy, green skin and the breath of cheap wine and spoiled cheese. Her dingy black outfit consists of a dress and cape ensemble. She gets right up in Rob's face and points her finger. She says, "You want to know the truth, well here it is. You caused your father's death, you miserable bastard. You did not help out enough around the house. His heart gave out because of your laziness. There are a million ways you could have saved him and it is my job to inform you what they are. I will not rest until you are fully tortured by the words I so brutally deliver."

Rob is frozen by the witch's harsh message. She is the voice of Supreme Guilt, the feeling of tremendous, all-consuming guilt that can never be erased or atoned for. He wants to move away from her, but cannot find the strength to do so. Words like machine gun fire and spittle fly onto Rob's face. She continues, "Why aren't you crying? Are you aware that you are the only member of your family who has not shed a tear? How can you not show any emotion at your own father's funeral? What are you, some kind of robot? Don't you have any sense of respect? Can't you even fake tears? Get back in the limo, you useless loser. Guess where you are going now."

The graveyard is below heavy power lines that sway in the cool wind. It is filled with decaying tombstones, ornate and simple, of various shapes and sizes. The cemetery is not frightening or consoling. It is numbing, a bone chilling stillness that knows neither time nor emotion.

24

The Gravediggers are methodically shoveling dirt out of the way for Rob's father's casket that is being carried from the limousine. The Gravediggers are not in tune with the solemn theme of the day. They seem to be unconcerned with Rob's father, mother, sister or anyone else. Rob asks one of the Gravediggers if this hole should have been completely dug out hours ago out of respect for his family. It seems rude to have this work done now, as the graveside service is about to begin.

The Gravedigger throws down his shovel and laughs at Rob and his family. "Respect," he says, "Why should I have respect for you, who are you? You are not important like these big tombstones over here with all the flowers in front of them. Respect. You can kiss my ass."

The casket is resting on the ground until the Gravediggers complete their task. Rob is standing next to his mother and sister. He feels estranged from both of them. They both seem totally unapproachable. His mother is wearing a dark blue outfit. Her eyes are red from days of crying and her face is haggard from the sudden loss of her husband. Her head is bowed to the ground. Rob wonders, "Should I comfort her? How do I do that?"

What can he say to ease her pain? Does he echo other empty phrases he has heard today? "Every thing will be all right, just give it time." "At least he was not in pain." "It was God's will." No, those words seem infinitely meaningless. Maybe his mother should be comforting him, but why should she want to comfort someone as horrible as her son had turned out? He has never seen his mother look so disturbed before, and he feels utterly powerless.

His sister is two years younger than he is. She seems crumpled and alone as her arms hang heavily by her sides. It is a burden just to lift her head and move her feet. She is crying buckets of tears. Why is he the only one not crying? Is this good or bad, right or wrong? He wonders what role he should play with her. The death of his father must be even more difficult for her than for him. Should he attempt to help her, or would she just tell him to leave her alone? He does not really know much about his sister and gives up on ideas of how to connect with her.

The Gravediggers haphazardly lower his father's black coffin into the ground. They toss it in like it's all in a day's work. Rob yells at them and requests that they be gentle. He is concerned because none of the mourners seem to share his outrage. The gravediggers hold their shovels in front of them

25

like microphones and begin to sing. "What is death anyhow? How can you live and die without a Jewish name? Is death a time to be merely tossed into the ground? Death is numbing, endless and unforgiving. Death is when your father leaves one day without notice. Death holds no answers for those who are undeserving. Death is isolation. Death is all anguish and without hope. Mr. Death is the Grim Reaper who arrives for the end of the funeral. He is a faceless, ghastly entity whose sole purpose is to take you out."

The Gravediggers unceremoniously shovel the final grains of dirt on his father's coffin. It is all so surreal to him. This is not really happening. This is a nightmare that will end as soon as he wakes up. His father is not really dead. How could he be? He must have gone to Vermont to visit his birthplace. Rob just saw him the other day having breakfast. He can't be dead. He can't be gone. No way.

Rob and his family crawl back into the limo and head for home, a home that will be a dismal place. He is totally demoralized, confused and broken. His nerve endings have become anesthetized. He attempts to look into the future and all he sees is darkness. Life will never be the same again.

COMMENTARY
Chapter One - *FUNERAL DAY*

MAJOR CHARACTERS
The Rabbi played by Lex Luthor
Supreme Guilt played by the Wicked Witch
The Gravediggers played by men shoveling
Death played by The Grim Reaper
Rob, Mother, Sister played by human figures

This first sandtray was built almost twenty-five years after my father's death. I was astounded by the realization that I had never fully experienced his funeral. That is, my experiences of his death up to this point had been incomplete. During the course of the previous twenty-five years, I had developed at least two versions of what happened that day. Throughout my life, I would focus on the story line that provoked the least amount of pain. One version was that I was numb and in a state of shock, and that is why I did not demonstrate any feelings on funeral day. The other was that the funeral was facilitated in an outstanding manner and all my needs were met.

I felt that there was something terribly wrong with my grieving process, but I was afraid to really look directly at my father's death. The "numb and state of shock" version of the story was that my visual memory of that cold gray November New Jersey day, the temple debacle and the lowering his casket into a hole, encompassed my entire experience of his death. At different stages of my life, I believed that the visual memory, devoid of any feeling was all I took from that day. This story line was one of detachment and isolation.

Over the years, I created an idealized version of the funeral that enabled survival and nothing more. The established story was that I was emotionally present from the day he died until now. I was attuned to my mother and sister's needs and did my best to help them. I was connected to their suffering and was clear on how to ease their pain. I was strong because I showed no emotion, no tears, and no requests for help. Furthermore I was not angry, sad, or conflicted whatsoever. I was shame-free and without guilt. The Rabbi was beyond reproach and his words were soothing to the ears. The funeral was an uplifting moment that launched my healing and eventual recovery. In this version, I was totally aware of the hurt inside my chest and the numbness of my heart.

This version was created in order for me to believe that I was indeed grieving properly and that I was "normal." I was unable to face my father's death in a more direct manner. What were the reasons for this self-deception? Why was it so difficult to face this tragedy? These questions began to be answered in this particular sandtray.

My long held versions of the first days after his death were now beginning to crumple and expand at the same time. They were beginning to crumple because I was realizing that these versions were created to protect me from the shock of a profound loss. Using these story lines as a starting point, I was able to expand on what happened on funeral day.

I was able to face several new truths. I was not clear about my role in the family. I was confused about whether and how I could help my mother and sister. I was internally frozen as the Gravedigger lowered my father's casket. My body and mind were infiltrated with hideous, intensive guilt. I was not emotionally present, and I had checked out long before that awful day. The

27

Rabbi's words were worse than silence, and they triggered self-loathing and chaos within. His words reinforced my disdain for organized religion.

The Rabbi sneered at my family when he asked, 'Did your father/husband have a Jewish name? ' This question and his ghastly reaction to the negative answer was so appalling, reactionary and hollow. Why was having a Jewish name so important? Why did the Rabbi seem to give this issue more priority than anything else? The fact that he did not know my father or any of us made the situation that much more surrealistically evil. He did not care about my father's life and he showed no empathy for the loss we were experiencing. The memory of this incident sticks in my gut because the Rabbi made me feel that my father, and all my family for that matter, were not of equal value to other Jews who had Jewish names. In other words, since my father was not religious – none of our family was – he did not measure up to the others who regularly attended synagogue. This encounter with the Rabbi trampled on my already low self-esteem.

I carried vague remembrances of this spiritual shattering throughout my teenage and adult years. Fierce energy was channeled towards forcing them into hiding. I wanted to bury them deep in the ground where they would never touch me again. Denial, minimizing and avoiding were the techniques utilized in protecting myself from this deep psychic injury.

I was introduced to several major characters that played leading roles. The figures of Rob, the Grim Reaper, the Wicked Witch (who was Supreme Guilt), my mother and sister brought substance and meaning to my inner world. I discovered the different aspects and levels of each character. Confronting and inhabiting these characters was so much richer than merely thinking or talking about the funeral.

The significance of these figures is a unique aspect of Sandtray Therapy. I could choose the figures, place them anywhere in the tray and look at them for as long as I needed to. Their physical presence held my attention and encouraged forgotten memories, misplaced thoughts and hidden feelings to emerge.

What benefits were obtained through facing the figures? I confronted the belief system that I could not and should not look at what happened when my father died. It was not a simple task to pursue, but the container of the sandtray gave me a sense of safety that had previously been unknown. In other words, since they were "just" figures in a sandtray, I could imagine their thoughts and share their feelings without being afraid those thoughts and feelings would overwhelm me.

I discovered a sense of relief at this newfound ability to look at a more complete version of the funeral. I learned that my father's funeral was indeed, not a cathartic ceremony that released my grief. The funeral was a numbing, bone chilling event that enhanced my unwanted separateness. The funeral was not experienced as a finalization, but as a confusing march into hell, filled with guilt and anxiety. I now saw the funeral as a real, traumatizing scene, not some hazy, pumped up vision of closure. I met the Grim Reaper, took in his essence and knew I was staring at death. Yet, I could now be with that scene and not push the flurry of terror away. I now welcomed the opportunity to re-experience my father's death in future sandtrays.

FAMILY DISCUSSION QUESTIONS
For Chapter One - *FUNERAL DAY*

1.   In the beginning of this chapter, Rob is so angry and out of control that he smacks his hand through a window. Have you ever had similar experiences?

2.   Music plays a large role in Rob's life. How does music affect you?

3.   Alienation and isolation are major themes in this chapter. Have you ever felt alone, separated or different in this way?

4.   Funeral day was the worst day of Rob's life. What have your funeral experiences been like?

5.   Rob meets the demons for the first time in this chapter. Have you ever come face to face with your demons? What are they like? What do they say?

6.   Rob feels cut off from his mother and sister during this chapter. He also feels confused about what his role in the family should be. Have you ever felt cut off from your family? Have you ever been confused about what role you should play with them?

7.   Rob feels guilty because he did not cry at his father's funeral. Have you ever felt guilty for not crying when you think you are supposed to?

8.   The Gravediggers in this chapter say to Rob at one point, "Why should I have respect for you? You are not important like these big

tombstones over here with all the flowers in front of them." What are the social, cultural and class messages here? What do you think about them?

9. Rob feels that death is numbing, endless and unforgiving. What do you think about death?

10. Rob does not feel that the religious aspects of the funeral were helpful. In fact, he feels that they were abusive. How do you feel about religion, religious services and rituals? Are they alienating or comforting to you?

CHAPTER TWO

THE ELECTRIFIED FENCE

CHAPTER TWO

THE ELECTRIFIED FENCE

Rob wakes up after a fitful sleep where night terrors fill his dreams. The spring sunshine pouring into his bedroom does not bring him warmth. The linoleum floor is cold to his bare feet as he hunts for clothes to wear. He does not care what he wears anymore. He used to like to eat, but food tastes like plastic forks.

He was supposed to be feeling better now. Six months had passed since his father died. He discovers that he is more despondent than ever. He decides that he will spend this Saturday walking around town. He desperately wants someone to help him out of his malaise. His mother is too sad to assist him. The teachers and guidance counselor do not seem to care if he lives or dies.

Rob takes the long way to the cemetery. This will be the first time he has visited the graveyard by himself. The headstone has finally arrived from the Veterans Department. It is small and lies flush on the ground. The grass has grown in and there are leaves on the few trees, but there is no comfort, only desolation.

Rob steps closer to the grave. Suddenly a man who closely resembles a gross monster steps in front of him. His eyes are bulging out of his head. His fire-like breath nearly knocks Rob over with its unearthly stench. He dares Rob to get any closer to the grave. He says, "Don't you get it? You are not supposed to look at death." Rob is paralyzed by the Monster-Man's short speech. The gross Monster-Man laughs so much he doubles up. Rob's stomach is jumping up and down. The Monster-Man is laughing because Rob does not know what is going on around him and cannot anticipate what will happen next.

A friend of the Monster-Man, Mr. Gremlin, stands beside him. He says to Rob, "I know you think I am a pointless, ugly old man, but I have a purpose here. That purpose is to scare the hell out of you." Monster-Man's laughter goes off the decibel scale. He continues, "I want to teach you a lesson about death you will never forget. You think Monster-Man and I are hideous. Wait until you see who will join us."

Rob is terrified. He has never seen these two characters before. What are they doing here? What do they want? What will happen next?

A man who looks like a green snake begins slithering around. He is about seven feet tall, skinny as a rail and poisonous as sin. He tells Rob that he is going to suck his brain out of his skull. The Bat Men that follow wear rancid capes and have vermin hanging from their lips. "We are going to totally destroy you if you don't play by our rules," they threaten.

Rob says, "What rules are you talking about? I don't know what you want from me." Mr. Death, the Grim Reaper, stands in front of the grave. He has a long robe and a hood hides his facial features. He says, "The world is all about death. Death has no mercy. It comes swiftly without warning. Death is numbing and forever. Life is meaningless. Your days are numbered, boy. I hungrily await your demise. Welcome to the Land Of Death".

Mr. Death tells Rob that he has a small present for him. He wheels in a box covered with black wrapping paper. He violently rips the paper off to display a small casket. It contains the skeleton of a little child. He yells out, "This is you. You died along with your father. You no longer have the will to live. You lost your ability to feel and you lost your sense of purpose."

Who should show up now? The witch called Supreme Guilt, who else? Her skin is green and her teeth decrepit. She tells Rob that he is on dangerous ground. She bellows, "Let me tell you the rules of death, you fool! First of all you should not even be looking at your father's casket. You see what happens when you do? You get confronted with Monster-Man, Snake Man, Bat Men and the worst of all, me. Don't you get our message? Do not look at death. Do not talk about the subject. Do not even think about it. Just leave your father's death alone. The best path you can take is no path. Just forget about him and go on with your life."

A person dressed as a clown; a jester, stands beside the gang gathered at the grave. He is laughing hysterically at Rob's ineptness. He is laughing at Rob's unwillingness to accept Supreme Guilt's rules for dealing with death. He tells Rob, "Don't you get it, if you forget about his death, it will eventually go away. You don't need to grieve; there is no such thing as mourning." Rob wonders if he is hearing the real truth today.

Rob picks up some black stones. Each time he does so, he is reminded of how stuck he is in The Land of Death. He places the stones near the casket and they seem to confirm the belief that he is stranded in this evil world, the Land of Death, forever. There is no resolution. There is no dealing with death.

A man with a pale face, sharp incisors and a regal cape comes out of nowhere. He is Dracula Man. His arms and legs have no muscle tone. His lips are blue. It is his job to enforce the rules of dealing with death. He says, "Young man, if you continue to look at your father's grave, you will pay a steep price. We will inflict ungodly pain on your soul."

Rob takes a step forward. He asks himself, "Are the demons telling the truth about the rules for facing death?" He gazes at the grave and all these evil characters surrounding it. Suddenly Supreme Guilt and Dracula Man install a gigantic fence around the grave. He notices that the fence is electrified and he will be fried if he touches it. Dracula Man says, "I supposed you are wondering what is the purpose of the electrified fence. It is designed to keep you away from looking at death. You will not benefit from all the sadness that this encounter with dying will bring. You will be destroyed if you get too close to the smell and decay that the ending of life brings. Listen up to this critical warning! If you dare to touch this fence, you will experience a powerful shock that may kill you. Keep out!"

Monster-Man keeps taunting him, calling Rob weak and gutless. Dracula Man continues to recite the rules. Supreme Guilt says, "Rob, you are such a parasite, are you too dumb to learn anything?"

Rob ponders that question as he attempts to block out the demons' continual barrage of scorn. He is pushed into a corner and feels the demons forcing him to not only obey their edicts, but to embrace their ideology. He feels pressured and frightened, but he is able to step away from fear for one second and consider his options.

From the moment his Dad died until now, Rob has believed that he was stuck in the Land of the Dead. Do the demons really rule his existence? Do they have control over every aspect of his life? Does he have to stay in this hell and listen to their dreadful speeches? Who gave them the right to make these edicts? Does he have to stay in this prison? What will happens if he leaves?

The droning speeches continue as the sun begins to fall out of the sky and nightfall descends. Rob pivots his feet and runs out of the graveyard. He hears Supreme Guilt scream at him to come back, but no one comes after him. He sprints as hard as he has ever run in his life. He stands in a clearing; sweat dripping down his face.

He rests a while and contemplates what just occurred. "Hmmm, I left and I am still in one piece, free from their evil influence. Let's see what happens if I return to their world. What will the demons do and how will that affect me? He walks back into the Land of the Dead, and the demons continue to yell cruel insults at him. He is no longer frightened, and their words seem to bounce off.

He exits the Land of the Dead once again and this time he does not run, he walks until he reaches a tranquil park. He sits down on a swing and is still for a moment. Then he swings back and forth until he soars so high; he can see the Land of the Dead. He realizes that he can enter and leave that evil world whenever he wants. He can enter and leave any place whenever he wants. As the swing reaches the peak of its arc, Rob smiles.

COMMENTARY
CHAPTER TWO – *THE ELECTRIFIED FENCE*

MAJOR CHARACTERS
Monster-Man played by Three-Headed Monster
Ugly, Old Man played by The Gremlin
Snake Man played by The Snake
Bat Men played by Bats
Death played by the Grim Reaper
Supreme Guilt played by The Wicked Witch
Dracula Man played by Dracula

In this sandtray, the graveyard was developing into a place of learning. The demons taught me society's myths of how to handle the death of a loved one, reinforcing my depressed state. This dysfunctional belief system is one that is ingrained in society's institutions and was certainly branded into me.

Large green fences were erected around my father's coffin. The Wicked Witch sang out her ironclad dictates, her rules of dealing with death. Her words

35

reinforced society's insistence on denying the reality of death. "Facing death is just plain wrong and taboo. The word grieving does not exist; it was mistakenly placed in the dictionary. Mourning is not helpful and will only stir up emotion, tears and anger. Besides, no one wants to be bothered with your anguish."

The Witch's overall, brutal message was "the most effective method of handling the death of a loved one is to not think about it, period. It is best to forget that he ever lived at all, just push the picture of his face out of your mind and go about your business. Do not talk, cry or think about death."

Dracula, the Grim Reaper and other demons were brought in to insure that death would not be faced. They laid out the dangers that will rain down on all those that disobey the witch's rules. They declare that our world is all about death, that death is forever, and life is meaningless. For years, I followed this ideology and paid severe price.

My demons had plagued me for as long as I could remember. They were yelling, screaming and belittling beasts. The slimy ones controlled every move I did or did not make. I believed that I was stuck with their presence when they stomped into my life. Now, the demons were invisible threats no more. They had shape, color, and names as well as voices. I could either listen to their hate filled soliloquies or walk away. I had a choice in this matter! I could enter the Land of the Dead and leave whenever I desired. I now had the option of accepting or rejecting society's myths about how we are supposed to deal with the death of a loved one.

FAMILY DISCUSSION QUESTIONS
For Chapter Two - *THE ELECTRIFIED FENCE*

1.   Rob felt a lot of time had passed and he didn't know why he still felt overwhelmed by the death of his father. Have you ever felt like this?
2.   The demons teach Rob not to look at death. What have you been taught about looking at death?
3.   The jester tells Rob that grieving is not helpful. Do you agree with this? Why or why not?
4.   At one point in this chapter, The Wicked Witch asks Rob if he is too dumb to learn anything? Has anyone ever said anything like this to you? Has it affected how you feel about yourself?

5.   Rob leans that he does have choices in his life. Do you feel that you have choices? What are their limitations?

CHAPTER THREE

A DIFFERENT WORLD

CHAPTER THREE

A DIFFERENT WORLD

The high school smells like a combination of old socks and teenage lust. It is two o' clock in the afternoon, and the students are restless and worn down by endless routine. Rob is in the auditorium that doubles as the study hall. He is sitting in a rock-hard wooden chair taking in the sights around him. Some of the kids are passing notes to each other. Some are talking and laughing in small groups, with their eyes looking out for the hateful glare of the hall monitor. Other kids are actually studying, reading and vigorously writing. Rob stopped studying long ago. Giving up seems like his only alternative. He is so far behind that it is impossible to catch up. He shrugs his shoulders at the red F's on his report card. His mother sometimes yells in desperation. Other times she gives up as well.

He stares at the second hand on the big clock. He hears it tick, tick, tick. He waits with great anticipation. At 2:40 exactly the bell rings and students rush in mass to the school's exits. A couple of his friends invite him to the sweet shop to play pinball, smoke cigarettes and wait for the girls to show up. Rob begs off because he wants to be alone.

He heads out the school's main door and walks deliberately for miles. He jogs into a meadow that is filled with clover, covered with late afternoon mist. The sun is peeking through the clouds on this cool, spring afternoon.

A black, heavy metal box appears before him. Could this be his father's coffin? It is so difficult to visualize what he looks like. He attempts to visualize what his Dad looked like when he was alive. He wonders what he looks like now. No visual pictures of his father light up the screen. The inner theatre is dark.

Rob reaches for a shovel that lies nearby. He begins digging the thawed out earth. The continual digging calms him. It is a mindless task that helps raise a sweat on his back and underarms. The repetitive placement of the shovel in the ground and carrying dirt elsewhere feels tranquil.

Mr. Doom interrupts this peaceful moment with his striking presence. He wears a dark maroon robe and hood ensemble. Doom's face is cobalt blue and his eyes are bright white. He pushes Rob away from the casket and the small recess he has dug in the earth.

Mr. Doom has a wicked smile plastered on his face. He says, "You do not learn, do you boy? You are supposed to stay away from this here death box. I know how to grieve correctly and you obviously do not." Rob asks him, "What am I supposed to do? What is the right way? Please tell me." Mr. Doom harshly stares at Rob, but does not utter a word as he turns and walks away. Rob shakes his head from side to side. Another adult who has the answers, but refuses to share knowledge. That is not what he needs right now.

Supreme Guilt takes Mr. Doom's place in the meadow. She has a black witch's hat and cape. Her long dirty fingernails are pointed at Rob. Her slimy green skin smells like burnt toast. She says, "You are the lowest form of life that has ever existed. You never cry for your father. You never show any remorse or sorrow. You do not offer to help your poor mother and sister. They are in such pain. All you think about is your miserable self." She pauses and then she introduces The Hunter with his shotgun. He is wearing a striped shirt and winter cap. He has a grim expression on his face and he is silent with impending violence. The witch yells out, "The Hunter can blow you away at any time, but you will not die instantly. You will suffer slowly in order to pay for all the damage you have caused."

Rob's heart is beating at a dangerously high rate. He almost hyperventilates because he forgets to breathe. He concentrates on the essence and words of Supreme Guilt. He says to himself, "She is right, I am a worthless son. I am selfish and thoughtless." Rob hangs his head in shame. He believes that Supreme Guilt's diatribe is gospel truth.

Mr. Death, the Grim Reaper stands near the hole in the ground. He is dressed in a silver gown and his face is the shadow of darkness. He says, " I watched as you dug this hole. Did you intend to bury your father's casket today? What are you doing? Are you trying to replicate his funeral? Why would you want to do that? I am not going to allow you to continue." He holds his position between Rob and the coffin crosses his arms across his chest and silently dares Rob to defy him.

Mr. Death sings a tuneless dirge. The melody is annoying and without structure or rhythm. Rob remembers his father's burial. The gravediggers were actually tearing up the ground during the ceremony. Some damned ceremony that was! There was no dignity for his father. He was pushed into an opening in the ground. Whatever legacy he had was lost forever. There were no words of kindness or hope. There was no uplifting grace. There were no stories told about his life.

Rob's attention is diverted towards a decades-old brown bridge. He hears a swooshing sound, like an avalanche. However this is not a prelude to disaster. It is the sound of skies gliding down a snow-covered mountain. The Skier is fearless in his black outfit and goggles. He is oblivious to all that surrounds him. He makes breath-taking turns and jumps.

Rob can make out the Skier's face, although a red scarf covers his mouth. He recognizes the Skier's posture and the intensity in his eyes. The Skier is his father. Rob longs to reach out to him, but knows that this is impossible.

His father loved to ski. Rob remembers pictures of him hanging in the air, suspended above the world. Although it was never talked about, Rob knew his father experienced freedom on the slopes.

He never saw his father ski when he was alive. His father never took him to the slopes. He is sad when he realizes that he will never have the opportunity to ski with him. The bitterness rolls to the front of his tongue. He spits green phlegm on the ground.

His moods are so erratic and sudden. The Skier continues to fly down the mountain. Rob yells out, "Nobody can steal this memory away from me, nobody. Mr. Doom, Death, Supreme Guilt, you can all rant and rave, but you cannot destroy what I remember."

The meadow has been turned into The Land of the Dead where the demons howl and the graveyard chills. Beyond the brown bridge live the Skier and the Calm Woman. She is African-American. Her skin is the color of rich coffee with a touch of cream. She sits on the ground with her legs tucked underneath. She does not worry easily, and panic is not part of her repertoire. She does not judge Rob at all. She does not blame him for his own misery. He instinctively trusts her. She says, "I am the queen of this world. It is different from the Land

41

of the Dead. This is a world of brightness, understanding and life. There is so much to be discovered."

A teenager with blond hair is running just below the mountain. He loves the feeling of being alive while lost in the adrenaline high of intense exercise. Rob recognizes the teenager. It is like looking in the mirror. The Runner speeds up from a jog to a sprint. His running celebrates the joy of living. The Skier honors his love of life in the same manner.

The Skier glides intensely through the snow as he faces the Runner lunging forward on the other side of the trail. They love the cosmic rush that exercise brings. They are both relieved at finding a method for getting outside their heads and finding respite from unmerciful thoughts. Rob feels like he is touching his father's skin now. Time stands still. He connects with his father's enjoyment of just being alive.

An older African-American woman is smiling and Rob feels brightened up by her facial expression. He feels like he has known her for a million years. But she is quickly fading away; she is dying of brain cancer. "Don't leave," yells Rob. She waves at him with a painful, yet peaceful look. She says, "I know you are smart, I know you can make it in this world, I love you." As she continues to fade away, she points to a multi-colored castle that is behind the mountain.

The Castle is majestic, made of blue, brown and layered yellow shades. It has a blue steeple and a glistening diamond near its top. The Castle belongs to this different world, the World of Life. So, what happens inside The Castle? Dreams are encouraged and created. The path to dreams is followed no matter how difficult the obstacles are. Sometimes dreams even come true.

Rob says to The Calm Woman, "The day my father died, dreams ceased to exist. I lost my faith in dreams and innocence. Dreams are not allowed in the Land of the Dead. It is in the World of Life where dreams can flourish."

The brown bridge connects the two worlds together. Rob is overcome with joy that he can leave the Land of the Dead and enter a warm, wonderful world, ready to be explored.

COMMENTARY
Chapter Three - *A DIFFERENT WORLD*

MAJOR CHARACTERS
Mr. Doom played by Hooded Blue Faced Monster
Supreme Guilt played by The Wicked Witch
Hunter played by himself
Mr. Death played by The Grim Reaper
The Skier played by himself
Calm Woman played by the African-American Woman
The Runner played by himself
Older Woman played by the African-American Woman

The discovery from the last tray of having choices leads to the unfolding of The World of Life. This is the first sandtray that includes figures identified as possessing goodness as their main quality. Those figures included The Calm Woman, The Castle, the place where dreams are created, the brown bridge that bridged the Land of Death and The World of Life together; and the Skier who was my father enjoying life.

Finding the World of Life broke through my belief that no such place existed. It helped lead to the knowledge that I had an inner world, a knowledge that was also brand new. Finally, discovering the World of Life opened the possibility that I could heal from spending too much time in The Land of the Dead.

I discovered I could connect with my father's love of life through rigorous exercise. That is something we share. When I created the sandtray scene of my father skiing through the snow, I felt as if I was touching his skin. Ever since he died I had been searching for a connection with him. I did not know how to begin to accomplish this feat. Now I could embrace this part of him, which helped me begin to understand him.

I also got in touch with the sadness I was carrying about my mother-in-law. She died of brain cancer and I was very close to her. Feeling this sadness led me to hope that I might one day feel my deep sorrow about my father's death.

Finally, I started to connect with the power of dreams and aspirations. I had been too numb and too hurt to dream before. In the next sandtray, I deal more with my dreams, and my father's.

FAMILY DISCUSSION QUESTIONS
For Chapter Three - *A DIFFERENT WORLD*

1. Rob's high school routine became boring and mundane. Did you ever feel this way about your school? Why?

2. Rob's did not do well academically in school and his grades were mostly F's. What are your grades like? Why are you motivated or not motivated to do well in school?

3. Rob notices that his moods swing abruptly and sometimes without reason. Do you notice that your moods changes can be erratic? What is this like for you?

4. Rob attempts to visualize his father when he was alive. Do you ever try to attempt to see something inside you and discover that you cannot conjure up that image?

5. Rob runs into Mr. Doom, a character who seemingly knows answers that will help unclog Rob's confusion. However, Mr. Doom refuses to share that information. Has this ever happened to you?

6. Rob realizes that he can connect with his father's love of physical activity. Describe the process of connecting with a peer and an adult.

7. Rob starts to the importance of dreams in this chapter. Talk about how dreams and aspirations are important to you.

CHAPTER FOUR

THE FATHER'S DREAMS

CHAPTER FOUR

THE FATHER'S DREAMS

The carnival is in town this week, and Rob walks down the hill from his house to the town's park. He sits by the river on a cool spring afternoon as the sun warms his face. The river is muddy and possibly the most polluted body of water on the eastern seaboard. Dead minnows wash upon the shore and abandoned shopping carts float downstream to nowhere.

Rob hears music coming from the carnival site. He can see the whole park from his vantage point and is curious about what will be performed at today's show. A magician is the first act and he wows the audience by making objects leave and reappear. Rob hears the crowd gasp and cheer over the magician's enchanting power.

The sky suddenly clouds up and the muddy river becomes turbulent. The wind begins to howl and screech. The Wicked Witch, Supreme Guilt flies on her broomstick across the water. Her moldy green skin blends in with the disgusting sludge of the river to invent a new color scheme. She lands in the shallow water immediately in front of him. Although Rob has faced her before, he is paralyzed with fear and does not move from his place on the riverbank. She does not greet him or give him time to collect his thoughts. She delivers another one of her messages designed to inspire self-hatred.

Mr. Doom quickly joins the witch near the shoreline. His pin-like eyes are like laser beams as they fixate on Rob's eyes. He says, "You out to have a good time today? How dare you? Your future does not include laughter or peace. Do you feel frightened, boy? Well, you should, because you are sentenced to live your life in a continual state of fear. You can moan all you want about your plight. No one really cares about you. Your cries of terror will never be heard."

Rob is filled with guilt and anguish as an African-American woman, Calm Woman, sits next to him. Her presence is calming and her warm, brown eyes comforting, as sand from the beach builds up around her and Rob, serving as a shield from the two demons.

46

Rob feels protected by her soft strength and firm resolve. He wants to tell her about what he is experiencing. He wants to tell her how scared he is and how he is filled with guilt about his dead father. He wants to tell her that he does not feel safe anymore. He wants to tell her that he feels so lost and alone. But, he will not say a word because he is still afraid she will sit in judgment and damn him just like the demons do. No, he just better continue keeping this misery to himself.

Rob allows Calm Woman's quiet to fill his insides for a moment. The storm that just brewed up has caused the temperature to drop twenty degrees in ten minutes. It's starting to snow big flakes and snowdrifts. He hears a whisshing sound, the sound of skis gliding down a mountain. He sees his father smiling, his face all aglow, the essence of happiness. He is not scowling or brooding like he usually does. His lips are not turned down in an eternal frown. No, he is ecstatic, enjoying life. Rob wishes that his father had been happy when he was alive. Rob feels his throat become tight and his breath short. Tears begin to form on his cheeks. He now knows that his father did have some joy in his life, but Rob is sad because he did not have time to share that happiness with him.

Rob walks away from the river with his head bent down from exhaustion. The weather is fickle today, and this fluke of a storm ends as suddenly as it begins. The temperature begins to rise again. He decides to go towards the carnival grounds where people are laughing and having a good time. Many have brought picnic lunches, which they eat on blankets spread on the lawn.

Rob continues walking through the crowd of people relaxing in the park after working hard all week. He sees a mom and dad, both in their mid-twenties and obviously enthralled with the infant in-between them, The Happy Family. The parents are smiling and coaxing the child to walk. This is the first time he has ever gotten to his feet, and he begins to walk. The father's whole being lights up like a rocket. The mother grabs a handkerchief to wipe her tears, acknowledging one of life's big moments. This is an occasion where all her prayers have been answered and time has stood still.

Rob steps closer to these young parents and their little boy. He is shocked to discover that they are his parents and the infant is he. He calls out to them, but they are in a world of their own. The longer he allows himself to be embraced by this family's interaction, the more clearly he realizes that his parents truly love him. This is a celebration of the goodness his family possesses. This is also an observance of unconditional love, a love Rob is very surprised to have wandered into.

Rob talks to the man of the family even though he knows the man cannot hear him. He feels warmth towards him and says, "Dad, you gave me the drive to finish a project, and you passed on your love of sports. You gave me a sense of family and along with my mother, you gave me the greatest gift of all, the gift of life."

A stone covered bridge is being laid across the river, linking the world together as one. Rob looks up as this structure is miraculously created in a few short moments. This connection leads Rob to experience separate parts of the park coming together. Mr. Doom and the Wicked Witch have vanished. Fear and confusion are replaced with serenity. The muddy, polluted water suddenly becomes crystal blue.

As Rob stares at the water, he notices a casket slowly floating down stream. He frantically asks the magician to assist in hoisting the casket onto the middle of the bridge. Rob now sees the casket up above for the first time ever. This new placement of the casket opens up a view of the future. He raises his head to take in this sight and he is suddenly transported to his high school, two years later.

He is wearing a cap and gown with a high school diploma in his hand. It is a hot, stinky night in the gymnasium. He feels disconnected to all the school administrators' droning speeches. This disconnection is not only from boredom, but also from the new method he has learned to numb his senses, narcotics. The graduate is so stoned that he can barely walk and has difficulty carrying on a conversation. His grandparents thought he was nervous or sick. His mother knew better.

Mr. Death makes an appearance at the graduation ceremony. Rob wonders if any one else can see his hulk-like body. The drugs have helped numb Rob out and pushed the pain away. However, nothing can prevent Mr. Death from coming into the world. Mr. Death says, "I am waiting for you to join me in this gray, cold lava and quicksand world of everlasting death. You seem to be doing a pretty good job at hastening an exit from life"

Rob's mother is screaming. She is ashamed of his behavior, but as she rants and raves, she realizes that she lost whatever control she had over him a long time ago.

Although Rob sees that the next couple of years will be difficult, he does not know how to alter this revolting course.

After this glimpse into the future, Rob is returned to the river, bridge and casket. The ghost of his father stands on the coffin. His father passed on many of his strengths to his son. When his father set out to accomplish a mission, he did so with a determination so powerful that it was all consuming. Rob now understands that this determination did not develop in a vacuum, that his father passed it on to him by example, by being a role model.

Rob walks away from the bridge and sees his mother, sister, father and grandparents. They are relaxed, so peaceful together. Then the grandparents leave and The Shadow of Adolf Hitler shows up with all his abusive power. He is ghost-like, transparent, which serves to tone down his unbearable hatred. When his father becomes angry, he turns into Hitler. Rob turns his back and escapes Hitler's wrath. He is so afraid of being yelled at, belittled or beaten.

Rob feels worn down by the abrupt changes during today's journey. The highs and lows come so suddenly that he barely has time to catch his breath. He walks back towards the water and approaches a beautiful, art deco castle. Rob knows that castles are often the holders of dreams. Rob does not know what the castle holds for him, but he is aware that his father had many dreams. Some came true; others never came to fruition. He dreamed of having a family and that one came true. He dreamed of owning a garden supply center, but he died before that could be realized. He dreamed of his son getting good grades in school, being a successful student. That was one dream that died on the vine.

Angels majestically walk into the river. They are happy, golden dreams that are also part of Rob's father's reality, his love of music. The clowns join the angels in the now pure water and play the harmonica and violin, two instruments Rob's father loved to play. One clown accompanies them on piano, which Rob's mother loved to play.

Rob sees the Statue of Liberty in the distant haze. He remembers how happy his father was to drive his family on vacation past the George Washington Bridge, past the Statue of Liberty, past the roadways of New Hampshire.

Rob sits down next to the fresh water where fish can now live without fear of extinction. He ponders many questions about his father, his death and what he is supposed to be doing about it. What beliefs should he embrace? What ideas should he discard and ignore? How can he say good-bye to his dad when he has never really said hello? How should he grieve?

The magician quickly hops on the casket, raises his arms and says; "We thank you all for joining us in the celebration of the life of Rob's father. We will share our memories of this man. We will talk about what was exciting to him and how deeply he cherished his family. Finally, we will talk about his dreams. After all, dreams are the center of a man's life."

COMMENTARY
Chapter Four - *THE FATHER'S DREAMS*

MAJOR CHARACTERS
Magician played by himself
Supreme Guilt played by the Wicked Witch
Calm Woman played by African American woman
Happy Family played by themselves
The Elderly Couple played by themselves
Mr. Death played by The Grim Reaper
The Shadow of Adolf Hitler played by himself
The Graduate played by himself

In this sandtray, I explored my father's existence on earth and determined that a celebration of his life was required now, because one never took place at his funeral. I learned that I acquired my drive to succeed from my father. This shared drive was another way to connect with him. I experienced his dreams and the sadness that comes from feeling that some of them did not come to fruition.

Although that insight was upsetting, I also was relieved to get a sense of my father, the man and what he believed in. He valued having a loving family the most. This was his highest priority. I touched on the fact that my father was both physically and emotionally abusive. I would learn later how profoundly this affected me.

The casket held other facets of my life besides my father's body. Memories, feelings and the creation of false belief systems were buried in the casket. In this sandtray, I was able to release bottled up feelings and memories, in the forms of The Graduate, The Happy Family, The Elderly Couple, and Hitler. The bottling up of these memories and feelings led to my state of numbness. Now I was releasing the pressure in this bottle. The bottling up was my family's rule for dealing with inner pain. Now I was beginning to break that rule.

The use of the bridge was a monumental step for me. The bridge elevated my father's death from the depths of the original funeral to a celebration of his life. At the same time, I knew there was a rough road ahead, as demonstrated by the graduation scene.

The bridge was also experienced as a way to connect worlds or parts of myself together. I was able to tolerate the coming together of the good and evil. For example, The Happy Family and Hitler stood next to each other. I was beginning to be able to experience the good and the bad simultaneously

The Happy Family and Hitler came into the sand for the first time today. The Happy Family is an introduction into my early childhood. Hitler is of course the epitome of evil in the world. It is also the rage in my father.

FAMILY DISCUSSION QUESTIONS
For Chapter Four - *THE FATHER'S DREAMS*

1. Rob gets in touch with guilt and self-hatred in this chapter. Have you ever had these experiences? Talk about them.
2. Rob cries in this chapter and the tears seem to come from a place of sadness and joy. Can you relate to this experience? Talk about it.
3. Rob discovers a loving family during his journey in the chapter. Have you ever encountered a loving family? What was it like?
4. Rob learns about unconditional love here. What does this term mean to you?
5. Rob talks about his drug experiences and how they altered his senses. Talk about what you know about drugs.

6.   Rob learned that his father passed on his sense of determination to him. What have your parents passed on down to you?

CHAPTER FIVE

HE'S NOT COMING BACK

CHAPTER FIVE

HE'S NOT COMING BACK

Rob is walking down Main Street and the town is quiet except for the ruffling of the quilt gowns worn by the borough rulers. The King and Queen make their entrance in their usual boring fashion. Their expressions are identical, flat and emotionless. They are reluctant to let down their respective guards. They refuse to be spontaneous or have any fun. They glance at Rob as he walks past and then quickly turn away. He is a nuisance that attempts to stir up controversy with his questions about life and death. Why can't he just shut up!

The King and Queen summon The Bitter Witch to put a stop to Rob's belly aching. She arrives with broken teeth in the front of her mouth. Her clothes are threadbare and her broom has few bristles left. The Bitter Witch reviews the rules of facing death once again and the words cut to Rob's core. She chants, "Do not feel pain. Do not cry, grieve or mourn. Do not feel anything but the coldness that surrounds your very soul."

Rob stands his ground and is rewarded by being left alone, without even the Bitter Witch's words to keep him company. Only the King and Queen remain, and when Rob looks into their eyes, he can see a sorry reflection of his own guilt, self-loathing and recrimination.

As Rob reaches the supermarket, he sees a Boy with Three Heads carrying bags of groceries to his car. The Boy is supposed to be his friend, so he offers to drive him home. They end up in Rob's back yard next to the tomato plants and weeping willow trees. It is now summer and Rob and the Boy are drinking lemonade.

The Boy works hard at earning Rob's trust. One of his heads gives Rob a series of compliments designed to boost his self-esteem. The moment Rob relaxes and lets his guard down, one of the other heads says, "You moron. I will tell you anything you want to hear. I will tell you that you are smart, a great athlete and popular with the girls. I will tell you that I am your best friend and that you can always count on me. But, the second your guard is down, the moment you relax, I will tell you the truth. The truth is that you are stupid.

54

You're an uncoordinated charlatan who should never play sports, and most of all you are ugly all the way through. My friendship is a lie. I hate you so much that I go to great lengths to bring humiliation to your soul. My only desire is to wound you. When you need me most, I will vanish into the air." At that moment The Boy with Three Heads turns into a fire-belching monster who breathes his flames in Rob's direction. Rob tosses the lemonade at him and runs into the forest.

A large antlered moose comes charging towards him and luckily Rob jumps out of his path. The moose would have killed him if he did not move in the last second. Rob does not feel safe in the world. His hometown alternates between ignoring and attacking. It seems like everybody hates him, even the animals.

He sits down on a log as a gorgeous pink flamingo lands next to him. She has long legs that look skinny and fragile. However, her long legs can run quickly if she is in danger of being preyed upon. She can briskly leave a perpetrator in the dust. She is a beautiful creature, but after recent events he has great difficulty accepting her beauty as being real. Is this a trick? Will she suddenly turn into a giant spider and try to kill him? It is difficult for him to believe that true beauty actually exists in the world. He fears that the tranquil feeling that the pink flamingo brings can be taken from him at any time.

A crawling baby with bright yellow hair is moving towards Rob. He knows that the baby is not real, that this infant is a figment of his imagination. The blond baby is Rob. He is innocent, laughing at the sky, tossing up the earth. He has not learned to fear life yet. He did not have a father who suddenly died one day and left him to fend for himself.

Two hobos join him in the woods as the baby vanishes. This man and woman have been living in the woods for years. They live for bottles of Thunderbird, Bali High, and Mad Dog. They ask Rob if he would like to share their libations and he does not hesitate to take a long swig out of the brown bag. God, it tastes like a combination of cough syrup and turpentine. Rob looks at the hobos and he is aware of the depth of his connection with them. They are laughing and carrying on like all is well, but this is just a false front to hide the self-hatred that lives inside. What was he doing here? Was he trying to escape his pain by getting high or was it worse than that? Was he attempting to join his father in his coffin? The hobo woman is mumbling incoherently. She really has no personality. It has been burnt out from years of substance abuse. All this

55

drinking and partying is phony. It is a false celebration because there is nothing here to be happy about.

Rob is despondent as he walks out of the forest and discovers himself standing next to the car his father drove on that fate filled day. He sits down on the curb, puts his head to his knees and bellows tears like a geyser. He is all alone, without friends, allies or adults to give him a helping hand. He is desperate to crawl out of his misery, but does not know how. He extends his arms to the sky and asks for help from somewhere. He begins to pray, and this is scary because he has never prayed before. "Please help me. Please let me know why I am so alone."

His prayers are answered, but he does not receive the comfort he pines for. Instead, the Grim Reaper stands next to the car. The reaper is solemn. He is mysterious without meaning to be. Death can take you out at any time.

Rob runs toward the ocean where he finds Neptune. He is strong, adventurous and kind. Neptune says, "I have been watching over you and I know that today's journey has been gut-wrenching. Come with me, I will lead you to a place where you may find peace."

Rob follows Neptune to the cemetery and his father's casket is all alone in the middle of the graveyard. Rob begs, "Please Neptune, take me away from here. I cannot bear to look at this coffin one more second. Oh, I so much wish he was here! Where is my Dad? Please come to me. Stop hiding! I know you are out there somewhere. Don't leave me all alone. I cannot live like this. Please walk out of that coffin. Stand up! Stand Up!"

Silence is the only response to Rob's anguished cries. He stares at the coffin in anger and seeks out Neptune, but he is long gone. Rob looks at the coffin and suddenly his hope for his father's resurrection dies. Tears wash down his face in a flood of torment and understanding.

He takes a deep breath. Rob begins to speak, "What is the truth here? The truth is that my father is really dead. He is never coming back and he will never ever be a part of my world again. He is dead. These words are neither an illusion nor a nightmare. I no longer have to struggle with this question. He is gone and it is now time to face reality."

Rob notices a small black casket with the lid off in the far corner of the graveyard. There is a boy in the coffin. It is hard to tell if he is breathing or not. Rob knows that the boy is he, and that he died the day his father did. A Bald Eagle flies near Rob's head and eventually lands near the small coffin. The Eagle is majestic and he can overcome any obstacle. His wings can soar a million miles per hour. He can overwhelm his enemies with brute strength and he can lend his power to the weak and demoralized. The Eagle's wing flapping has caused the boy in the coffin to come alive. He is coming to life after so much time being dead, numb, exhausted. The little boy finds the power to walk out of the casket and slowly walk towards Rob. Rob holds out his hand to the little boy. They both scream with joy when their fingers touch.

Now Rob decides that it is time for true celebration. Clowns march down the river and celebrate the acceptance of the death of his father and the re-birth of Rob. All the townspeople show up. Even the dour King and Queen crack smiles as music plays.

A Wizard stands on his father's coffin and he asks for a moment of silence to recognize the life and death of his father. Rob bows his head in quiet reflection.

Adolf Hitler, The Holy Family and The Skier join the party. Rob realizes that they are all parts of his dead father and all deserve recognition. Rob tells the crowd, "Hitler was my father's rage. His anger simmered inside. The Holy Family is what my father cared most about, and The Skier was his freedom."

The party begins to wind down as the gravedigger with his shovel moves towards his father's coffin. It is time to bury him. Rob asks the gravedigger for his shovel and digs dirt and piles it on top of the casket until it is completely covered. He sits down on the ground with sweat and dirt all over his body. He lets out a big sigh of relief and says, "I can finally bury him because I know now he will never be coming back." He sees a black cloud lift off of his shoulders. The little boy runs up and says, "I can let go of the guilt I have held so long. I did not kill him. I had nothing to do with his death. An illness took him that November afternoon."

COMMENTARY
CHAPTER FIVE - *HE'S NOT COMING BACK*

MAJOR CHARACTERS
King and Queen played by themselves
Bitter Witch played by herself
Nymph played by himself
Three Headed Boy played by himself
Pink Flamingo played by herself
Crawling Baby played by himself
Hobo Man and Woman played by themselves
Mr. Death played by The Grim Reaper
Neptune played by himself
Little Boy in Casket played by himself
Holy Family played by themselves
Skier played by himself

In this sandtray, although things are still hard for me and for Rob, you can see the weight of bottled-up guilt and fear lifting. I felt free enough to place figures at random. I did not get stuck in feeling that I had to create a good land versus an evil one. In the end of the tray, I was able to bridge the whole thing together. I experienced that my father was really dead. I felt this loss throughout my body, not just my head. I was able to genuinely mourn my father's loss. I was able to cry and experience deep grief. I got in touch with different aspects of my father's life. I talked about what I felt I was missing now that he was gone.

I found a place where such truths can be told. This is a place where total silence is tolerated and confusion vanishes. When I told my truth, that his death was not my fault, I discovered and experienced a way to dispel my guilt and shame. This major development demonstrated my progress in the sand. This place where truths are told is known by many names. The psyche, the place of inner wisdom, and the place of higher truth are a few of the ways this phenomenon is described. The major gift I received today was that I discovered my psyche, and I relished it.

The tears on my face helped me fully experience my father's being dead. I had not realized that, by numbing myself in self-defense, I had missed out on this crucial experience. The reality of the sadness gave me a sense of inner security that I had not felt before. Feeling, hearing, and sensing that he had died opened the door to my psyche.

In this sandtray, I saw that my father's abrupt death had caused me to mistrust everything. At age 15, the thought of someone's dying, much less my father's dying hardly occurred to me. Suddenly he was gone, and that meant there was open season on all my previously held beliefs about the security of life. I could not trust the beauty of the Pink Flamingo. Was she real, and most of all, would she stay?

The Three-Headed Boy dealt with my experience of no longer trusting the words of friends. The swiftness of my father's death led me to doubt any praise offered by friends or adults. At fifteen, I began to not only doubt their sincerity, but also believed their kind words were only temporary moments of respite from the hatred they felt towards me. I believed that life was a bitter joke, that nothing good would ever last and that fear and suffering was what the experience of life was all about.

Like Humpty-Dumpty, I was putting myself back together again. This bridging the fragmented parts was leading me to inner truths. It also was preparing me to immerse myself further into the dark side, where more demons would be experienced.

FAMILY DISCUSSION QUESTIONS
For Chapter Five - *HE'S NOT COMING BACK*

1. In this chapter, Rob experiences his hometown as extremely boring. How do you feel about the town you live in?
2. Rob has a difficult encounter with a friend in this chapter. As a matter of fact, he feels betrayed by the Three-Headed Boy. Have you ever been betrayed by a friend? Talk about it.
3. Rob realizes that he does not feel safe in the world. Have you ever felt like this? What has it been like?
4. Trust is another big issue brought up here. Talk about the importance of trust in your life.
5. Rob experiences loneliness in this chapter. What happens when you get lonely?
6. Rob realizes that his father is really dead and will never return. Talk about an experience that is similar for you.

CHAPTER SIX

THE ROSE COLORED HEART

CHAPTER SIX

THE ROSE COLORED HEART

It is four A.M. central Jersey time, and the air is filled with the dung of humidity and bad memories. Rob is tossing and turning in his bed, half listening to the local rock and roll station playing The Ronettes, The Crystals and Dion for young insomniacs. He throws the covers on the floor and goes to the bathroom. As he turns on the light, he sees a frightened face in the mirror. His eyes are without water and his skin is the color of old bleached out white sheets.

He returns to his room and puts on his old blue jeans and decides to drive the Comet, even though it will be at least a year until he obtains a driver's license. He defiantly lights a smoke as he starts the car. He hopes his mother is still asleep, but he does not care if she hears him or not. She has given up trying to control his erratic behavior. She has given up on raising him altogether. At least, this is how it seems.

The car seems to have a mind of its own as it takes the familiar path to the cemetery and parks in front of his father's headstone. The sun is beginning to rise and is peeking through the late summer clouds that flood the horizon.

Rob looks closer and finds himself all alone, and it feels like he is the last person alive on the planet. His father's casket lies on top of the ground, and there is no hole for it to be placed in. The casket and headstone have been eroded from the torrid summers and harsh winters that New Jersey brings. The weather-beaten headstone has his father's name and the dates of his life etched on it, although Rob can barely read the faded letters. As the sun continues to rise, more headstones become visible. They are made of granite, gloomy and finite. This is the place where all energy comes to its demise because this is the end of the line.

Rob finds a shovel nearby and begins to dig a hole for his father's casket. He feels like his head is inside a vacuum and he hears a tornado twirling between his ears. It sounds like trains are colliding in his frontal lobe. Why is he back at the grave? Why is he burying his father again? He remembers how awful the real funeral was. The memory of that day makes his blood begin to boil with sheer rage. The hole in the ground is deep enough for the casket to be placed and to be covered. It is chilly and damp in the dug up earth. The pungent odor of the wet earth permeates his sense of smell. Nothing moves here. He is confused about what he does and does not have power over. Does he have power over what happens with his life? Does he have control over what others do with their lives? Did he have power over his father's death?

As Rob shovels dirt into the ground, he is in turmoil. He finds it so easy to blame himself for all that has gone wrong. His face is scrunched up in agony. He says, "It is the same old grave. Why do I keep coming back here? I must enjoy torturing myself. It is just a metal box in the middle of a wasteland graveyard. I keep looking for answers. I always end up beating myself up. Does anyone else keep returning to his or her father's grave? Why do I keep repeating this act?"

He surveys the cemetery. No wildlife can survive these conditions. He feels distant from his surroundings. He feels the numbness. He is trying to keep evil buried. Every time he returns to the graveyard, he can focus on the darkness and craziness. He has tried to clamp down and keep the evil out, but he has learned that this is impossible. Evil needs to see the light. Evil needs to be faced, not repressed. Rob realizes that he has been working hard at pushing the dark side away. He has used almost all his energy at keeping the evil at bay.

He feels too exhausted to finish burying the casket and is now sitting by the headstone. He stares at the dates of his father's life, and suddenly anguish replaces the quiet. He asks, "Why did he have to die? Why did he leave me? Why did he leave me all alone? Oh God, why did this have to happen? I am so lost." Tears ride down his face like the Comet racing to points south, along the shore. It feels like a dam that has been holding back an ocean for hundreds of years has finally broken loose. All Rob's grief is now flooding the earth.

A slight wind blows through, and the leaves on nearby trees begin to rustle and fall. The leaves are burnt orange, bright yellow, and scarlet red. What a beautiful sight! They are celebrating the seasonal cycle rather than focusing on what is dead or dying. The trees shout out, "He was a good man. He didn't have a Jewish name, but he really did not need one. Those who loved him did not care about that. He worked hard to insure that his family was taken care of. He loved them all so much."

The headstones have changed from moldy slabs filled with morbid death images to multi-colored stones that honor a man's life. His father's headstone is the brightest one of all, and it can talk. It says, "It was so difficult for the family when he died so abruptly. He was here one minute and, without warning, gone the next. It is time to acknowledge and honor the pain that his son carried for so very long. What an overwhelming struggle it has been. We, the headstones hereby recognize this family and bow down to express our wonder at how courageously you have faced this indescribable loss."

Rob is surprised that his father's coffin is now totally buried. He must have completed the job without knowing it. His father's headstone has changed again. What do we have here? It has been transformed into a rose colored heart. It is his heart. He has found his heart!

Rob is so choked up that it is difficult to find his voice. After several minutes, he looks at the rose colored heart and says, "Dad, I want to tell you that until today, I never really cried for you, not from my heart, because I simply did not know how. I did not know how to begin mourning your death. Your very presence was the anchor of my life. When you died that anchor was forever cut adrift. I never felt safe or secure again. You have no idea how much I miss you."

Bright yellow flowers are placed on the grave, as they are the plants of sadness. It is so sad that his father was not able to say good-bye to all those who loved him. Rob is in touch with the blame, guilt and agony he has carried for so long. He is amazed at how much he weeps and how he is no longer afraid of the sadness. He is suddenly aware that the sadness, when allowed to flow its natural course, is a healing force, not a destructive one.

COMMENTARY
CHAPTER SIX - THE *ROSE COLORED HEART*

MAJOR CHARACTERS
No other characters

In the sandtray, Rob was able to become more human today. He became less stiff and more lifelike. I was able to ask for the first time, why did my father have to die? This opened up the grieving door inside me.

I had been aware that flowers were placed at gravesites as a ritual in this country. However, up to this point, I did not understand the purpose in doing so. I had believed that the flowers were like so many meaningless, hollow symbols of American life; that the crass commercialism of phony sentimentality sold many sympathy and greeting cards, expensive coffins and flower arrangements. I discovered that the flowers were meaningful, that they could assist me in grieving my father's loss. The flowers acknowledged all the sadness that was locked inside me. They honored my father's life with grace.

I located my heart. In my heart I got in touch with the deep sorrow I had been carrying around for almost twenty-five years. The sandtray not only helped me locate my heart; it enabled me to see it. I could hold it in vision and in words. I discovered the place inside me where life originates, the heart. I found the place where I feel pain, confusion and joy. I learned that sadness was a normal part of grieving and that the sadness would not kill me. In order to fully grieve, one must allow the sadness to come through. Grieving becomes "stuck" when sadness is diverted by shame or bitterness. The good news is that it is possible to transform this state.

FAMILY DISCUSSION QUESTIONS
For Chapter Six - *THE ROSE COLORED HEART*

1. Rob looks in the mirror and is troubled by what he sees. What happens when you look into a mirror?
2. Driving became an essential part of Rob's life. What do you like about driving?
3. Rob feels like his mother gave up on him. Have you ever felt that your parents have given up on you?
4. Rob feels frustrated and confused because he has returned to his father's grave once again. Talk about your experiences of going over the same thoughts and issues repeatedly.
5. Rob realizes he had been working very hard on keeping the dark side away. What do you think he means by this? Can you relate to it?
6. What are the purposes of a funeral? What needs to happen in order for these purposes to be achieved?

CHAPTER SEVEN

THE REAL MEMORIAL

CHAPTER SEVEN

THE REAL MEMORIAL

Rob drops the basket of fries into the boiling grease that percolates inside the smoke filled restaurant. The oil begins to turn the frozen potatoes into crisp morsels of teenage gourmet heaven. His white uniform shirt and apron are covered with hamburger renderings and coke stains, and it isn't even two PM yet.

Rob has been working as a short order cook in Katz's Knishes for several weeks now. He slaves over a grill during weekends and evenings during the week. He is also asked to wash dishes and slice onions until his tear ducts run dry. He makes $1.50 an hour preparing this glorified junk food for his classmates and the suburbanites recovering from all day jaunts to the swim club.

Rob's boss is a weaselly browbeater who is overly concerned with his shortness of height. His toupee never seems to fit right as he spits out racial slurs to all those he thinks agree with his self-righteous prejudice.

The boss checks the cash register and immediately accuses Rob of giving a customer too much change. Rob hurries over to his boss and slams the cash register with all his might as silver and paper money fly haphazardly all over the floor. His boss screams at him as Rob vacates the busy lunchtime restaurant. The boss begins to chase him, but realizes there will be no one left to cook the grease-laden food. Rob runs until Katz's Knishes is no longer on the horizon. He runs to a place that has become a comfort zone to him.

The cemetery is a welcome sight and now a place of quiet reflection. Fall trees of red, amber and gold form a circle on the outskirts of the headstones. Their trunks are strongly rooted into the ground and are indestructible, yet their leaves honor the passing of time. They pay tribute to the seasonal changes that life brings. Rob recognizes that the changing color and dying of the leaves is the actuality of autumn, winter, spring and summer.

Rob's mother and sister suddenly join him in front of his father's unburied casket. Even though they are standing nearby, neither looks at or speaks to Rob. His mother is pensive, downcast and gloomy. Rob was a difficult child to

66

manage before his father died. Now, he is absolutely incorrigible. He stays out to all hours of the night and he hardly goes to school any more. His mother's black hair lost its luster some time ago. For one quick moment, she looks him in the eye and sneers. There is enough hatred in the air to stop a World Series celebration in its tracks. His mother despises the very ground he walks on, and her anger is mixed with a profound sense of resignation. She has lost all control over him, and her washed out blue eyes admit utter defeat.

Rob moves a step closer to his sister and mother. They gasp in unison and abruptly back away from his advance. They are terrified of his rage, and they fear that he will physically harm them. His sister cowers against a tree as she tells him to go away. His mother attempts to protect her from Rob. He takes another step towards them and they immediately vanish. He hears them crying tears of terror as they exit the scene.

Rob sits down in the middle of the graveyard. He is ashamed that he has messed up so royally. His family is afraid of him; he is flunking every class that is offered; he now smokes up to a pack a day, and his future as a fry cook is in deep jeopardy.

He is lost in intertwining guilt and misery when he notices a bright red heart in front of the casket. The heart is Rob's and he feels the sadness his mother and sister hold. The heart is in agony as it takes in their pain. Rob says, " My sister lost her father and she is even younger than me. I feel so hurt, but she must be devastated. She deals with his death by hiding out in her room while I deal with it by lashing out at the world. My mother lost a husband, her partner for life. My god, what can she be going through?"

Rob is suddenly standing next to a bed inside a hospital and he is afraid to look at the man who is lying there. His father is very sick and is slowly dying, but Rob cannot face him. He turns his face away from the bed as he hears the nurse admonishing him. She is pasty faced underneath her ancient nurse's cap and she says, "You must leave. Only medical personnel are allowed in the intensive care unit. Can't you read, boy? Get out now." Rob defiantly holds his ground as the nurse goes on to harass some other innocent.

Rob tries to look at his dying father, but cannot face what the experience of death holds. He sees himself in his graduation gown, and he knows that his father will be unable to attend. He will probably graduate with a D-minus minus

67

average, way at the bottom of his class. He holds a nearly meaningless diploma, the gateway to a meaningless life without a father.

A football player and baseball catcher stand near the hospital bed and Rob feels anger bubble up inside. He wonders why his father, while highly competitive, would not let his son try out for teams he may not make. Probably, he wanted his son to avoid the pain of this group rejection. Rob wants to tell him that instead of sparing his feelings, his being unable to try out for sports made him feel inept, as his father must have felt when he was not good enough to make the rosters. He wants to tell his father this stuff, but cannot because he is in a coma now. He cannot hear Rob's words. He cannot stand or walk, he cannot talk and he cannot open his eyes.

Rob tries to look at his father in a coma, but realizes that he is not ready to accomplish this act. He briskly walks out of the hospital and offers an obscene gesture to his favorite nurse. He heads to the center of town where he encounters the Happy Family. A husband and wife are fawning over the baby as he begins to walk for the very first time. The father is so proud as he watches his son move his legs and feet. The mother is content and she is at peace with the world. The epitome of joy is caught in this moment.

Rob becomes overwhelmed with sadness when he realizes that he has no memories of his parents looking at him so lovingly. Did they ever have that strength of love for him? He searches his memory bank and comes up blank. That blankness leads to a feeling of numbness when he sees his mother and sister across the street.

Fortunately they have not noticed him yet, or at least, they act like they do not see him. They seem like wounded and frightened mannequins. He says to himself, "My mother and sister are dead. My whole family perished the day my father died." This thought causes Rob's eyes to tear up and he does not want anyone to see his pain.

Rob is back in the graveyard, and his father's coffin is on the ground near the open grave. Rob quietly contemplates what is going on in present time. He says out loud, "Wouldn't it be nice to create Dad's funeral the way I would have liked it to have been?"

He walks to his father's coffin and lowers it into the ground. He cannot find a shovel, so he scoops up dirt with his hands and he covers up the coffin.

He hears a rustling behind him so he turns around, and a large group of people are there, waiting for him to speak. He relishes his opportunity to conduct the memorial the way he would have liked to do it, rather than the crude, harsh version facilitated by the worthless Rabbi.

Rob brushes the dirt from his jeans and asks someone in the crowd for some soap and water to wash his hands and face. The cool water soothes the skin of his brow, and he begins to speak. He says, "My father was a good man, a fine man really. He wanted a family he could love, cherish and protect. He was more committed to this principle than any one I ever knew."

"He spent his whole life searching for a sense of wholeness, and when he thought he had almost attained it, he became sick and then abruptly died. He left behind a wife, son and daughter who to this day experience the intense loss of his drive, compassion and love of life. My father was a gifted athlete and was intelligent. I did not get to know him as well as I would have liked. Had I known that he was going to suddenly die, I would have rushed to understand his every complexity; I would have strived to make him laugh and to comprehend what made him cry. I would have hung on to every moment spent with him and never give into distraction."

"He loved the outdoors and music. He played the harmonica and violin with a joy that overcame the everyday worry he carried. He worshiped my mother, and I am certain that he would have fought a grizzly bear if he thought we were in danger."

Rob is finished with the memorial speech and he notices many members of the audience crying along with him. He then changes into his running clothes, laces up his shoes and asks one of his friends to light the torch he holds in his right hand. The torch is lit and its fire beams up to the now darkened sky. Rob yells out, "This torch honors my father's life and places the gifts he had in our hearts forever." Rob runs with his head up, and the flame of the torch lights up the town on a day that no one will ever forget.

COMMENTARY
CHAPTER SEVEN - *THE REAL MEMORIAL*

MAJOR CHARACTERS
Mother and Sister played by themselves
Dying Father played by himself
Graduate, Football Player and Baseball Catcher played by themselves
Happy Family played by Baby's First Steps

I discovered new rituals for the funeral experience. When building this world, I moved towards experiencing what a memorial service could be. I learned what the purpose of this ceremony was. It is the celebration of a person's life and the discussion of what was really lost. If my father's life had been celebrated at the funeral, it may have opened painful doors that in reality stayed shut for years. The aloof and cold atmosphere of the actual funeral contributed heavily to my being consumed with numbness. A celebration of his life could have reached my locked out heart. The fact that this did not occur is nothing less than a personal tragedy.

I was learning that it was helpful to revisit the original trauma. It was also healing to recreate the original trauma in the sand the way I wished it could have occurred. This gave me a sense of completeness. I was able to finish what felt so undone before. The original funeral did not help me say good-bye. It did not aid in my mourning. The original funeral left me bitter, numb and incomplete.

I had no idea that this re-creation would feel so liberating. I felt like a ton of weights had been lifted off my shoulders. If some professional therapist had told me that this technique would be helpful, I would have thought she was crazy. I would have believed that I was spending too much time in fantasyland and avoiding the real pain. But it turned out that as long as I could make the distinction between actual history and the way I wanted history to be, I was on the right path.

Being able to re-experience my father's death and recreate the funeral allowed me to bury his casket in the ground again. This is a clear sign that I have broken through the denial of death. While I had experienced the reality of my father's death before (for example, in the sandtray called "He's not coming back"), I was still far from fully accepting and integrating his loss. This kind of acceptance takes time and repeated efforts. Acceptance comes and goes away again. I had previously thought I had experienced his death as deeply as I ever would. I now knew better and had a sense that experiencing his death would continue in the trays that follow.

I had found my heart in the previous tray. This enabled me to bring my family into this one and look at our turbulent connection. I went deeper into my relationships with my mother and sister. It became clearer that I lost them the day my father died. I was immersed in guilt and shame, and I thought that I had mistreated them with my anger. These were difficult memories to explore. A sense of courage followed guilt and shame. I was becoming strong enough to confront these memories.

I realized that I was not ready to think about my father's actual experience of dying in the hospital. I had not been allowed to see him in the intensive care unit, and neither was my mother, although she did "sneak" in. His dying and suffering were more difficult to face because I was not physically present at his deathbed. It may have facilitated my grieving experience if I had been allowed to see him dying in order to make it real. I certainly advocate this for the majority of my clients.

His suffering and dying had also been difficult to face simply because I was not ready for the internal hurt I feared would come if I did. I was now at a place where I could face this knowledge and not be filled with shame. This led me to the belief that I might be able to think about his suffering one day, and that it would further strengthen my acceptance that he was gone.

I could connect with my mother and sister's sadness, but I could not actually communicate directly with them during this tray. I was not ready to take them into the heart of my journey because I needed to figure out my own pain first.

FAMILY DISCUSSION QUESTIONS
For Chapter Seven - THE REAL MEMORIAL

1. Rob has a job working as a cook in a restaurant. What kind of job experience do you have? What do you like/dislike about your job?
2. Rob gets into an intense confrontation with his boss. Has that ever happened to you?
3. Rob senses his mother's disappointment in him. Talk about how your parents express their disappointment in you. How does this affect you?
4. Rob's mother and sister are afraid of Rob's rage. Has anyone been afraid of your rage?

5. Rob discovers empathy towards his sister and mother in this chapter. Can you point out where in the chapter this occurs? Talk about your personal experiences with empathy.

6. Rob's father attempted to protect Rob from the cutthroat world of competitive high school sports. How would you feel if your parents prevented you from trying out for sports?

7. Rob recreates his father's funeral the way he would have liked it to be. Do you think there is value in recreating traumatic events in our lives?

8. Have you ever been in a hospital? Talk about that experience.

9. Has anyone close to you ever died? What was that like for you?

CHAPTER EIGHT

WE ARE ALL GOING TO DIE SOMEDAY

CHAPTER EIGHT

WE ARE ALL GOING TO DIE SOMEDAY

Rob looks around the cemetery on this crisp fall day. The trees loom large around his father's coffin, and their leaves are the brightest he has ever seen. The contrast of the bright yellow sun with the orange leaves lifts his spirits even higher. Rob notices a full-length mirror planted in front of him. He sees his reflection and for once does not turn away in revulsion. He sees a smile on the boy's face and his blue eyes are no longer dishwater dull. They are alive with the curiosity and optimism of someone who has survived a fierce, ugly storm.

Rob places yellow, purple and white flowers on the casket. For some reason, he does not feel the need to bury it today. He takes his time in experiencing the world surrounding him. He slowly picks up orange and yellow leaves that have landed nearby. He places them on the coffin and watches the beauty unfold outside and feels the warmth of his beating heart.

He is sad and happy simultaneously. He is sad that his father is dead and never coming back. He is happy that he has found the means to honor his father's life and mourn this terrible loss. The flowers, leaves and sun reflecting on the casket open up the pathways to facing his father's death in a way he would have never imagined before. It feels so good for the sadness to erupt in his heart and tears flow from his eyes. What was once numb, untouchable and surreal is now very real. This is not a cruel dream designed to torture him. No, his father is really dead and his son is all alone, but still alive with his future ahead of him.

Rob's mother and sister join him at the graveside. He does not notice their entrance until they are standing directly behind him. They are wearing the same drab clothes they wore on funeral day. They are depressed, broken and frightened. Rob does not believe that they will ever move from this state. He begins to speak, "I am feeling so alone. I lost a father. He was here one minute and dead the next. I spend so much time aimlessly driving around looking for someone to guide me, someone to hold me and say that everything is going to be alright, but that touch, those words never come."

He turns to look at his remaining family and thinks, but does not say, "You lost a husband and you lost a father. You must feel the same as me sometimes. I wonder what you do feel? I wonder if you feel as devastated as you look?" Rob does not dare utter these words because he is afraid what they may bring. He is afraid his words may be yet another dagger in wounds that will not heal. He is afraid that they will turn away from him and never return. If only he could find the means to reach them....

Rob turns towards the mirror and takes in his entire reflection. He says, "I am going to die someday. We shall all die someday." His own words startle him. He may have heard these words before, but had never faced their implication. Rob looks at his mere mortality and he is surprised that he does not run from this truth. He continues, "Death is natural as life is. Death is part of life, and life is part of death. This is truth, not a horror to be feared. The bright fall colored trees signify the end of summer and the beginning of winter. Death is part of the cycle of nature just as the seasons are."

Rob hears a loud fluttering behind him, a sound that he has never heard before. It is coming from the sky, but does not sound mechanical, or like any bird he knows. He suddenly sees two giant wings in the distance as the bald Eagle lands near the coffin. His head is raised majestically with utmost pride.

Rob stares at the Eagle and wonders how a species so beautiful and strong can be endangered. The Eagle is strong enough to survive years of human neglect and the purposeful killing known as hunting. Rob is puzzled for a moment and contemplates the human destruction of the Bald Eagle. It is true, he thinks, that life is part of death and death is part of life when death occurs naturally, but not when people purposely eliminate life on earth using instruments of destruction, without thought to the consequences. There is no license granted for randomly killing animals or people. Rob vows to keep the Bald Eagle alive.

COMMENTARY
CHAPTER EIGHT - *WE ARE ALL GOING TO DIE SOMEDAY*

MAJOR CHARACTERS
Mother and Sister played by themselves
Bald Eagle played by himself

I found a tie to my mother and sister. That link was the shared loss of my father. However, at this point I felt that it was impossible and hopeless to actually sit down and discuss the events of his death with them. I was beginning to wonder if their feelings and memories were similar to mine or dramatically different.

I got in touch with my own mortality and the knowledge that we all die someday. I heard the higher wisdom that death is natural and not to be feared, another step in breaking through the denial of death. Realizing that death is natural helped me tear down some inner defenses and enabled me to be less afraid of my father's demise. In each sandtray, the shades covering the windows of his death opened a bit wider. I was experiencing more memories, feelings and connections.

Our society tends to deny death and pretend that it is not natural or inevitable. This denial inhibits grieving and can keep survivors stuck in grief and mourning the rest of their lives. If the Rabbi at my father's funeral had sat down with me and stated the universal truth, that death is a natural occurrence, then perhaps I could have initiated grieving at that time, instead of going numb.

Death and life are part of the same natural cycle. This does not mean that people have the right to indiscriminately maim or hurt animals or other humans. This knowledge is reflected in Rob's concern for the Bald Eagle. And thinking about the limits of people's right to hurt others was the gateway to exploring the abuse and neglect that I experienced as a child. Delving into those memories takes place in futures sandtrays.

FAMILY DISCUSSION QUESTIONS
For Chapter Eight - *WE ARE ALL GOING TO DIE SOMEDAY*

1. Have you ever wondered what will happen when you die? Talk about it.

2. Rob talks about the senseless killing of animals. What do you think about this?

3. Rob says at one point that he feels all alone. Have you ever had this experience?

4. Rob finds a connection with his mother and sister, the shared loss of his father. What connections do you have with other members of your family?

CHAPTER NINE

SAINT MARTIN DE PORRES

CHAPTER NINE

SAINT MARTIN DE PORRES

Rob is driving the Comet at speeds not meant for winding, dangerous hill roads. He is reflecting on his latest report card. Days absent - 25. Days tardy - 18. Number of A's, B's C's - 0. Number of D's - 3. F's - 5.

A fresh cigarette is hanging from his lips as he attempts to assess his plight. The guidance counselor told him two years ago that he was too dumb to take college preparatory classes, but in defiance, he took them anyway and proceeded to fail. His fifth grade teacher told him that he was the dumbest student she had ever had during her fifty some odd years of teaching. At this moment, Rob is feeling as smart as a fuel rod. He does not think about the future because it does not exist beyond the next traffic light. He hears something sliding around in the trunk. It's probably car parts that have become dislodged from Rob's careless driving habits.

The snow on the ground is melting from this unusual warm winter day, and the icicles hanging from the trees are quickly turning to water. The glare from the snow and sun is decreasing Rob's visibility as he decides to stop on top of a mountain.

He has a view of the entire county from here. It is the same place George Washington stood as he watched for the enemy's approach. Rob could see his high school football field, the park and his house from here.

He turns around and is astounded to discover his father's coffin. "How the hell did that get up here? What is it doing here?" he asks. After a moment, he calms down and stops panicking. His father's casket is looking over the whole world now. It is overlooking the entire universe, and Rob is pleased that his father's casket is placed in such an exalted position. He connects with the coffin like never before. His father's life suddenly has meaning, depth and purpose. Being placed on top of the mountain honors his life in a spectacular way. He can look down on the valley below, and those living on the foothills can gaze up on him.

Rob looks across the plain and sees a small cemetery with six red headstones. The red is blood that has been spilled by the dying. The blood is the life that has poured out of them, and the headstones are a remembrance that the people buried underneath were once vibrant and alive.

A huge elephant with bright jewels hanging loosely from his body is walking near the bottom of the mountain. He is strong and oblivious to his surroundings. He is confident that he can protect himself from any predator at any time. He leaves footprints in the earth as he stomps about.

Rob wonders if he can ever match the strength and self-assuredness of the elephant. He wonders what it would be like to walk around with your head held high and not worry about being destroyed from the inside.

The haze of New Jersey has miraculously lifted and Rob can see for miles and miles. He can see New York City and parts of Pennsylvania. He turns his head from side to side, scanning the environment, preparing for any surprise attack. He must always guard against being blindsided by an unforeseen enemy. He can be injured or wiped out without notice.

He sees a deer running down the mountain with the grace that only a god could give her. The deer is adventurous, playful and inquisitive. Her desires are to run, eat and have fun. He worries that she will be shot by a half-witted hunter or killed by another animal. Rob wants to keep the deer safe, but he cannot control her travels. He cannot control a lot of what happens in front of him.

The Eagle's wings are flapping. He is a powerful bird. It takes tremendous strength to lift his wings. He is announcing that he has landed. He is proud of who he is. He is proud of his history. He will fight the forces that are attempting to totally remove his kind from the face of the earth. Rob wants to help, but does not know how. He is lost in this struggle.

He continues to view the valley below him as he turns his head from side to side during monotonous intervals. Oh-oh! All of a sudden he hears a bellowing, brain piercing scream. The Monster-Man is at the end of the trail near the bottom of the hill. He is truly a horrid, disgusting sight to behold.

His skin is the color of diarrhea and he is both tall and large. He holds a sharpened ax in his right hand, raised over his head in the attack position. His teeth are huge structures with dark stains embedded upon them. His incisors are sharp enough to cut through iron. His pointed green-yellow eyes pierce through in a psychotic glare. He is enraged at Rob for bringing the casket to the mountaintop. He foams at the mouth as he charges up the hill and says, "It is a crime to let thoughts of your father's death linger. They must be immediately eradicated! It is wrong and taboo to hold on to these thoughts and feelings any longer!" Monster-Man swings his ax, but he cannot reach Rob because he has found rocks to make a barricade, which protects him from this living disaster.

Christ hanging on a cross joins Rob near the mountaintop, and he has a pained expression on his face. His beard and hair are wild and unkempt and his eyes are rolling into the back of his head. He has been beaten and nailed to a piece of wood they call a cross. His body is past the point of hurting as his arms bleed from holes near his wrists. He is paying for crimes others have committed, they say. He is guilty of stirring up the people by talking about world peace and the horrors of war. He got strung up for talking about the cycle of life and death. He got crucified for talking about different ways of suffering.

Monster-Man tells Rob that extreme suffering is his fate if he continues to look at his father's death any longer. The Monster-Man yells a blood-curdling scream that can be heard for miles. Monster-Man's edict is harsher than even the Wicked Witch's words of warning. Rob says to himself, "The message is that if I face death or even utter the word, I face a slow, calculated, extreme kind of suffering before dying myself."

Rob runs from behind the barricade and somehow dodges the menacing Monster-Man as he runs down the mountain with the purpose of joining the jeweled elephant. Then a black man with a robe draped around him walks out from behind the elephant. He has long fingers and immediately disarms Rob by his calm smile and peaceful presence. Rob's heart stops racing as he takes in the energy of Saint Martin De Porres. He is the patron saint of the animals and the poor. Saint Martin can protect all those he loves. Rob has been looking for this all his life. He feels that he can place his trust in Saint Martin, but does not have a clue as to how to go about beginning this process.

Rob gets the notion to speak to Saint Martin and quickly admonishes himself for this dumb idea. He looks at Saint Martin, so serene with his black skin contrasting with the white collar around his neck. He thinks, "Maybe I can speak to him even though it seems forbidden to ask anyone for help. How could talking to him help? It seems so silly." Rob decides to casts these beliefs into the wind and blurts out, "Saint Martin, does the Monster-Man speak the truth about, umm, you know, about looking at my father's death?"

Saint Martin does not immediately reply, as his smile changes to an expression deep in thought then back to a smile again. He finally says, "What do you think young man? Is the Monster-Man telling the truth? Is looking at your father's death unhealthy? Will it lead to an emotional breakdown?"

Rob first reaction to Saint Martin is bitter disappointment. He mutters to himself, "Here is yet another adult who refuses to help me. I even found the courage to ask him for help, but he responds only in riddles and more questions. If no one will give me the answers, what am I supposed to do?"

Rob looks into Saint Martin's eyes as his bitterness turns to something else entirely. "Saint Martin is telling me to look inward for solutions," he thinks. He then pauses and resumes talking, "No, Saint Martin. The Monster-Man does not speak the truth. It is important to talk about my father's death. It is important to talk about my numbness, sadness, anger, and need to understand. If I do not express any thoughts or feelings about his loss, I will be stuck in perpetual numbness." Saint Martin tells Rob that he is right. He needs to face these things and talk about them, but doing so does not mean that the evil will disappear forever.

Two Angels of Death fly over the mountain and land near Christ. They honor his father's death by passing the word around the globe as they fly. They carry the sadness that was not felt, expressed or experienced the day of his death. They are beautiful creatures covered in gold and their wings flutter as they buzz around the mountain.

The Grim Reaper, Death, marches up the trail along with the devil as they stand directly in front of Christ. They chant and hum incoherently in a ritual designed to ensure Rob's loyalty to the old rules of not facing death. He turns away from their vigil.

After that, things start to move fast, too fast for Rob to understand what is going on. A lighthouse beacon shines nearby. This is a safe place for solitude and reflection, but there are too many mixed feelings emerging now. It is impossible to think about reaching the lighthouse.

A large, pearl handled sword is angrily plunged into the east side of the mountain near his father's casket. A silver tree with no leaves plunges into the earth. Black and red water are forming a lake below. Red is for life and black is for death. Rob's mother and sister are attempting to walk up the mountain. "No. Go Away. I cannot deal with your anger and despair," he says. He knows they cannot hear him because they are too far away, but they abort their climb and stand transfixed.

A treasure chest floats up from the lake and it holds the promise of a better life; a promise that Rob does not believe at all. The Skier glides in front of Monster-Man. He is spiritually alive and untouched by the range of emotions surrounding him. The Calm Woman appears behind the red headstones. Rob is glad she is here, but does not invite her to converse with him.

A hospital room with infusion equipment enters next and a headless man is curled into a ball on a bare bed. Flowers are placed on the casket as the action continues to accelerate at an alarming pace. Rob feels fear as the situation spirals out of control.

"There are so many mixed feelings and I am moving forward, backward, sideways as the evil ones, the demons are having their day," he says. Then another emotion takes over. He picks up the pearl handled sword and begins stabbing it into the earth near his father's coffin. He yells, "Why did you leave me all alone, so unprepared to deal with life? How could you have left me without knowing which questions to ask and with no one to ask them to? Why did you leave my feeling so full of guilt, shame and confusion?" He continues jabbing the sword into the ground until dirt is scattered everywhere. "Why didn't you tell me that you were going to leave? How can I help my mother and sister? How could you leave me alone in such pain? There is no one to comfort me," he says with faded voice.

Rob is exhausted and his rage worn down through his cries and stabbing of the earth. All that is left is this raw sadness. He feels a sorrow encompassing his brain, spirit and heart. He is naked, facing the tragedy of his father's death with no protection. He begins to put his shield up in order to prevent this anguish from tearing up his internal organs. But wait! The sadness will not destroy him; only the repression of it will cause him harm.

Sadness tells us that there is something to be mourned. Numbness blocks the sadness. If there is no sadness, there can be no grief, and so no healing. Rob is thankful for the tears that refuse to leave his face.

COMMENTARY
CHAPTER NINE - *SAINT MARTIN DE PORRES*

MAJOR CHARACTERS
Jeweled Elephant played by himself
Monster-Man played by himself
Jesus Christ played by himself
Saint Martin De Porres played by himself

St. Martin entered today. He is my voice of wisdom. In previous trays I had discovered my psyche and my heart. Now I had an inner sanctified entity to guide me. I trusted his words implicitly. I was not sure if he was a father figure, a god or a spiritual leader. It did not matter at this point. I felt I could trust him but wondered if I would really turn to him if I became troubled or confused.

Jesus Christ also entered today. He is the major icon for religion, suffering, love and the forgiveness of sins. The positive message of Jesus that I grew up with was that love could overcome hatred. I touched on all these aspects in this tray.

We are taught from a very early age to seek guidance and wisdom outside of ourselves. Looking inside for knowledge about how to face death and life was brand new for me. Instead of continuing to be bewildered, frightened or numb, I could look inside myself for answers. My internal wisdom figure could help me find them. It is my opinion that learning to trust your inner knowledge is the most magnificent gift the sandtray can give.

This tray might seem like a step backward, but it wasn't. For the first time, I got in touch with my rage, which is an essential part of grieving. The demons returned during this tray, but I did not let their return stop me. I was able to tolerate the combination of the demons and voices of higher wisdom. I was able to face the abrupt turns this tray took.

84

The rapid moving of figures and scenes came from some kind of intense feeling, but at first, I didn't know what the feeling was. Then I discovered the rage I felt for my father's dying. I got in touch with those angry feelings that were triggered by his supreme abandonment. It was not like he took a vacation and I could speak to him when he returned. No. He was dead, and I was mad as hell that he left me so alone and unprepared to handle what came after he died. After this anger was experienced, the raw sadness emerged.

I experienced deeper sadness and I found it was a gift; one I did not want to lose. I learned that sadness is essential for mourning. Sadness was not experienced when I was fifteen, only numbness. But now I was moving on to further challenges and further growth.

FAMILY DISCUSSION QUESTIONS
For Chapter Nine - *SAINT MARTIN DE PORRES*

1. Rob's guidance counselor told him that he was too dumb to go to college. Has any adult ever said anything like this to you?
2. Rob talks about confidence in this chapter. Do you feel confident?
3. What do you think it means that Rob's father's casket shows up on top of the mountain? How did it get there?
4. Rob feels like he must always guard against being blindsided by an unforeseen enemy. Have you ever felt this way?
5. Rob realizes that there are many facets of life he has no control over. Talk about control.
6. Monster-Man tells Rob that it is taboo to think about his father's death. What has been a taboo subject in your life? Have you ever wanted to talk about it and felt that you were not allowed to?
7. Rob feels comforted and supported by Saint Martin De Porres. He feels that Saint Martin is a wise man. Have you ever felt this way about anyone?
8. How did Rob feel as he was stabbing the dirt with the sword? Have you ever felt that way?

CHAPTER TEN

JUDGMENT DAY

CHAPTER TEN CONTINUED

JUDGMENT DAY

CHAPTER TEN

JUDGMENT DAY

It is fifth period, and while the majority of kids his age are in vacuum packed classrooms, Rob is in the Fourth Avenue Sweet Shop dropping nickels into the slots of the dimly lighted pinball machine towards the back of the store. The sounds of pinball mix in with rock and roll that is being piped out from the jukebox where 45's play endlessly.

He starts to gag when the chorus of a happy Beach Boy's song is belted out. What is there to be happy about? Where is all this fun that they sing about? He is filled with melancholy, because no matter how much new stuff he learns about himself, he still feels stuck in desolation and anguish. He is confused about what is happening to him, and the bewilderment is driving him to a hollow apathy. He is totally convinced that no other kids, and certainly no adults have any idea what is going on inside him, nor do they care how alienated he feels.

He tries to bang the sides of the machine to get the silver balls to hang on the sweet spot of the levers, but his hands are weak and stiff and the ball drops in the hole at the bottom of the machine. Silence, the game is over. As he digs into his pocket for more nickels, a witch covered with metal comes through the door.

She announces, "Today will be like no other, because today is your day of judgment. You must face all the demons that you so cleverly avoid. You are a coward who is too scared to walk up to those forces of evil that plague your every waking hour with taunts and recriminations. You cannot face them because you know deep in your heart that their words are an accurate description of your loathsomeness."

The Metal Witch coughs in Rob's face while the walls of the sweet shop seem to close in on his tired body. The atmosphere has changed from one of bored indifference to a penetrating evil. "Judgment Day", says Rob. "I am going to be tried by all the demons I have encountered since my father's death. They are going to hold me to a standard that I can not begin to comprehend or meet," he cries out to the empty shop.

88

The Metal Witch has left, but Rob looks out the front window and sees the reflection of a hooded figure. The face is hidden; maybe the man or creature does not have a face. Maybe all he has in its place is a shadow. It is the Grim Reaper, and he controls the music on the jukebox. The Beach Boys' sound gets slowed down to a funeral dirge.

The Grim Reaper, the lord of death now enters the sweet shop. Each step he takes corresponds with the soulless beats of the dirge from the jukebox. The air becomes thinner as the volume of the music rises. Death is in the air. Death is always in the air. Rob notices that The Grim Reaper is following some sort of dance pattern. He is lurching around doing a macabre cha-cha-cha.

Rob anticipates The Grim Reaper's dance step that has him momentarily facing the wall away from Rob. As soon as the shadow turns away, Rob bolts out the door. He runs past the Metal Witch with all the speed he can muster. She warns him that no matter where he goes, he cannot escape Judgment Day. It will envelop him like a swarm of killer bees attacking a naked intruder.

He finds the keys to the Mercury Comet in his pants pocket and starts the car up and zooms away. "Where should I go? What should I do?" he asks himself. He is keenly aware that the demons will catch up with him and when they do, each one will vilify, threaten, humiliate, demean and torture until there is nothing left of him.

He drives the back streets of his hometown killing time and making plans to deal with the looming doom and destruction. He passes familiar landmarks that include his friends' houses, the police station which is part of the demons' conspiracy, and the park He drives by the high school, even though school is in session and some official may spot him and turn him over to authorities for punishment. What can they do? Suspend him? Big deal, he never goes to school anyway. The worst punishment that could be handed out would to be locked in his music teacher's class and be forced to get up close and personal with her breath for twenty hours a day.

Rob is hit by a surprise attack of sadness, and tears flow onto the Comet's custom upholstery. He is so lonely, and he has no one to help him deal with the demons. How many hours has he spent driving around his hometown of one square mile searching for answers? How many times has he turned a corner hoping that something or someone would be there to hold him close and say everything was going to be all right?

89

He does turn the corner only to see his mother and sister walking down the street with their heads bowed in silent suffering. He does not want to, but he experiences them as demons because they hate him so much -- at least he thinks they do. They never come out and say that they despise him, but words do not tell the story here.

He stops the car beside them as his mother slowly turns her head and looks into his eyes. Her whole face is filled with disappointment, disgust and hopelessness. She holds no hope for her son. He is a dismal failure on all fronts. He is an accomplished liar and is prone to violence. She is afraid to talk to him about his shortcomings for fear of retaliation. She feels her own life is futile, and she is going through the motions of raising two kids whose needs she has no idea how to meet. His mother's look is worse than any beating could be.

Rob peels out, leaving smoke and rubber in his wake. He looks in the rear view mirror and is not surprised to see that his mother's expression has not changed. He drives until he ends up in the place that provides him the most comfort. He still has a difficult time believing that he finds the most solace in a graveyard, but he can't deny that reality.

Fog rolls in with the cold darkness of night. Rob is carrying a lantern that enables him to see his father's headstone. He walks toward his favorite spot when all of a sudden the demons sweep in. The Metal Witch, The Grim Reaper, The Raven Witch, The Headless Man, The Wicked Witch, The Three Headed Dragon, Monster-Man and his mother and sister surround him. He is trapped and the Metal Witch speaks of judgment day. She says, "I will not address you by name. As far as I am concerned, you have no name because you have no presence. You are an it, a thing that is in direct line to get blown to bits. I am going to reintroduce my fellow demons to you, and a number of them will express their sincere hatred of the ground you stand on."

First comes Monster-Man who says through puke filled teeth, "You are too weak to live. You keep wanting to discuss your father's death, which is a supreme sign of weakness. You must be destroyed."

The Wicked Witch is next, and she says, "You must never move from the place of keeping all your guilt and shame intact. You must hold this pain in your stomach, heart and head. You must never forget that you are guilty of not anticipating your father's death, not preventing it, and not consoling your

90

mother and sister. Finally you are most guilty of the crime of trying to rid yourself of the twin prongs of guilt and shame. This is intolerable, and your punishment will be swift and severe."

Rob waits to hear from his mother, but all she does is offer him a glance, that look that makes him want to curl up in the fetal position. But there is no time to withdraw because danger is in the air.

Rob feels a rage boil up in his stomach and drive straight to his pounding pulse. He looks at all these demons. He sees a sword on the ground and feels adrenaline rush through his body. He thinks about picking up the sword, but instead ignores it and moves closer to the demons. He runs up to the Monster-Man who is stunned by Rob's insurrection.

He pushes Monster-Man onto the ground and proceeds to repeat this act with every demon in his path. Rob's rage is running rampant and he hates death for not unveiling its mystery. He hates the endless sermon of "You are so bad, worthless, etc." He hates being stuck halfway in life and part way in death. He is so angry that his mother and sister do not empathize with him. He is angry that he did not have the chance to be with his father when he died, that he never got to say goodbye.

Suddenly Rob buries all the demons deep into the nighttime earth. He stares at the dirt covering his hands and says out loud, "I am free. I have found the will to fight against evil. I have stood up to the voices of hatred and self-loathing. I have crushed the myths of how to look at death. I turned the tables on Judgment Day."

COMMENTARY
CHAPTER TEN - *JUDGMENT DAY*

MAJOR CHARACTERS
Metal Witch played by herself
Grim Reaper played by himself
Monster-Man played by himself
Mother and Sister played by themselves
Supreme Guilt played by The Wicked Witch

91

The sandtray is a medium that teaches us how to face our inner demons. Before I began this journey, I did not know how to accomplish this fundamental task. In fact, I had no idea that I had a world living inside me. *The Electrified Fence* sandtray taught me that one way to deal with the demons was walking away from them. I discovered that I had the choice of facing the evil or walking away from it. This was an empowering experience that led to the action in *Judgment Day*.

I buried the demons in this chapter. Unleashing my rage and angrily burying the demon figures took me a step closer to the truth. The truth is that death needs to be talked about, cried over and grieved, not pushed down and denied. Anger is part of grieving, and I gave myself permission to allow my anger to unfold, to not be repressed any longer. Now I had two options in facing the demons.

I revisited shame and guilt. I blamed myself for my father's death throughout much of this sandtray world. Denying shame and guilt, when you have them, blocks you and numbs you the same way denying sadness does. I needed to experience the shame and guilt, because only then could I get in touch with the anger that these feelings provoked. And the anger gave me the energy and resolve to face the demons, cast them off and let them go.

We all have our own journeys. I learned that when I return to shame and guilt, a major learning experience will follow. Looking at such difficult feelings was scary, but not destructive. Facing shame and guilt in the tray is different than how I was overwhelmed by their piercing presence through much of my life. The tray was teaching me how to work through the guilt, rather than being stuck with it as I was in adolescence. The bridging together of good and evil, burying demons, and walking away from them were tools that I was going to need as I ventured deeper inside.

FAMILY DISCUSSION QUESTIONS
For Chapter Ten - *JUDGMENT DAY*

1.   Rob feels alienated in this chapter. Do you ever feel this way? Talk about it.
2.   Rob plays pinball in order to escape the harsh reality of his life. Do you ever try to escape? How?

3.   Rob talks about an unpleasant experience he has with his music teacher. Talk about your unpleasant experiences with teachers.

4.   Rob experiences emotional turmoil in his stomach. In what part or parts of your body do you experience stress?

5.   Rob is angry that his mother and sister do not empathize with him. Have you ever been angry with someone because they refused to step into your shoes?

6.   Rob feels ashamed through much of this chapter. Do you ever feel ashamed? What do you do about it when you feel that way?

7.   Rob believes his mother thinks he is a failure. Does he really know this? How do you know how your parents feel about you?

8.   The demons take turns attacking Rob and telling him how bad he is, until Rob reacts with anger. Does this scene remind you of anything in your life? Do you believe Rob could really silence the demons the way he did?

CHAPTER ELEVEN

THE GUILT POEM

CHAPTER ELEVEN

THE GUILT POEM

It is 3 AM in the dead of winter and the wind is shaking Rob's bedroom window. He cannot sleep, so he gets up and looks outside. Snowflakes quietly fall down past the street light on the corner. He is cold, agitated and alienated from the world that surrounds him. He feels soulless and empty, and he regrets the day he was born. He sits by the window, opening it up an inch or so in order to blow the cigarette smoke into the frozen night air.

This desolation is increased by the knowledge of what daybreak will bring. His mother is insisting that his whole family return to his father's grave later that day. Rob is very edgy about this one-year anniversary of his father's death. He is unsure of the point of returning to the cemetery with his sister and mother. He does not see how it will help him break free of the continual angst he lives with, this dark cloud that always hovers over him and engulfs him in a halo of guilt.

The brown Comet has been replaced by a French car that feels remarkably like a tin cup while riding on the highway on the way to the cemetery. Winter sure came early this year. There is a hard packed snow on the ground, and the roadways have to be negotiated carefully because of ice.

Rob is sitting in the front passenger seat while his mother is driving. She does not speak to him or to his sister who sits quietly in the back seat. Rob wonders if his mother is supposed to help him instead of making believe that he does not exist. He knows that she acts this way towards him because he is so out of control, so mean spirited that he does not deserve to be treated kindly.

On one hand, he desperately wants her to tell him that he will be OK someday. On the other hand, he hates the very ground she walks on. He does not understand how he can have both of these feelings. He wonders how he can hate her and need her so much at the same time. His anxiety rises as they get out of the car and walk towards the grave.

Rob looks past the headstone where a cave sits on a body of water. Two divers are swimming near the cave's opening and they are armed with spear guns. They do not want anyone to get near the cave. Rob wonders what they are protecting.

He notices that flowers have been placed on both sides of the grave. This is very strange because he can swear that the flowers did not exist a couple of minutes ago. He does not remember his mother or sister carrying flowers from the car. The bright yellow, orange and blue flowers contrast so beautifully with the white snow. Some how they give him hope that he can finally discuss his father's death with his mother.

Rob looks up again towards the cave, and he sees a husband, wife and baby standing close to each other, keeping each other warm. The parents are dressed in their finest clothes, and they smile with a love that stems deeply from the heart. This family is proud, secure in their posture and nothing can stop them from holding each other tenderly.

This family reminds Rob of a picture of him and his mother and father standing together. The three of them seemed so happy then. Rob tries hard to connect with the family by the cave, but he cannot. He is not sure if he ever experienced this loving moment in his life. What happened to him? Was the picture a lie? Is the family by the cave putting on a performance designed to humiliate him further? He can certainly see them so alive and connected with each other, but he cannot take their joy into his heart.

There is a small bridge to the left of the cave and it leads to a tall grandfather clock. Rob can hear it ticking. The ticks start slowly, and then speed up along with the adrenaline rush in Rob's brain. The ticks turn into bells tolling loudly. He wonders why no one else complains about the racket. Rob feels that time is not on his side; that he has to rush to some unknown destination for a pointless endeavor. He feels suffocated by time constraints that are placed upon him. He feels the pressure of needing to quickly find solutions to unresolved questions.

The Blue Faced Ghoul emerges from the inner most regions of the cave. He stands on the perimeter holding a small cat in his hands. Even though the Ghoul is across the water, his presence seems right in Rob's face. He stares into Rob's startled eyes and says, "You are playing with fire again my friend. How many times do we need to tell you not to look over here at the cave, not to take casual walks to the grave because... because YOU ARE VIOLATING THE RULES! By now you should know what rules I am referring to - The Rules of Dealing with Death. Some day you are going to cross the line and you will no

96

longer have a choice whether to follow these rules or not. Guess what will be your plight? You will lose your sight and hearing, and become so claustrophobic that you will scream to be let out of the box you put yourself in. But it will be too late because you will then be damned for all eternity."

Rob notices his mother on his left and his sister on his right as they face the casket. Rob's mother opens her mouth to say something, but all that comes out is a long sigh of pain, the agony that they all have experienced this past year. Rob does not feel the slightest connection with either of them. He assumes that they are really not interested in his plight, and he does not seem to know how to become interested in theirs.

Something is about to happen, because while he was not paying attention, moss and other greenery grew in near the upper banks of the river that flows in-between the cave and the cemetery. Something is about to happen because he can feel it in his bones. He does not know if it will be good or evil, but he trusts that whatever happens, he will be enlightened.

Two magicians of bronze and silver walk up to Rob and his family. Rob is happy to see them, but both his mother and sister have shocked expressions on their faces. The Magicians bring a sense of lightness to the proceedings, and their only purpose is to bring joy to their audience. They are kind and captivating creatures who are here today to celebrate the gathering of the family in front of the casket. It is one year later and they are still surviving. The Bronze Magician tells Rob that he is here to assist Rob with whatever pain he faces today. He says, "I am here to move the grief forward. I hope to lessen the burden of the dark cloud surrounding you." His sister turns her head and looks at the magicians. She does not understand the Magicians' gifts. She does not understand their purpose or knows how to benefit from them.

Rob begins slowly pacing back and forth and during each step he takes, his feelings deepen and intensify. All at once, he feels the freedom to make a decision on what voice to believe in. He trusts the words of the Magicians. He does not believe the Blue Ghoul's forecast to be accurate. He says, "I am seeing things I did not see before." He feels the sadness and joy deeper inside. As these feelings grow, everything around him starts to change before his eyes.

Another small bridge enters near the clock. More moss is planted on the right hand side in front of the casket. A bench is placed just in case any of his family wants to sit down during or after the gathering today.

97

A small piece of paper is placed in the teenager's right hand. The river that separated the casket from the cave becomes filled in with sheets of yellow, leaving a small pool for the divers. The divers no longer have to patrol. They now swim for fun. The river is mostly filled in now, with the exception of the small pool between the casket and cave. The pool is calming rather than warlike.

Rob says, "It's me, I have a poem. *I Am Not Guilty* is its title." He reads,
"I did not kill you. I did not kill you! I am not guilty!"
This is my poem for you, Dad.
Millions of times I have been obsessed with being guilty.
Bad stuff happens. I get scared, then paranoid.
My thoughts are just like yours.
You worried a lot. You always worried.
This whole way of thinking goes nowhere.
There is no solution, because I am always guilty.
I can never find redemption, because I put this huge burden on my shoulders.
It is a ritualistic, masochistic way of punishing myself.
My fantasy is to go to the grave, to feel clear and at peace, with my stomach not eating itself.
I beat up on myself everyday.

The teenager turns to the evil ghoul in the cave. "I will read this poem," he says. "I did not kill you, I did not kill you, I am not guilty! And I am prepared to face whatever wrath you give."

The poem is still grasped tightly in his hand. He needs to shout his feelings to the world, that he is not guilty of murdering his father. His mother and sister do not show how they feel about Rob's poem, but at least they do not leave.

He continues reading:
"I used to watch as you came through the door
every night after work.
You would sit down and hold your head
and demand that we be quiet.
You tried to play catch with me, but there was no fun in your eyes.
Only a pain that I never understood.
You got so mad when I didn't clean my room right.

You were so disappointed in me because I hated school so much."

"You took the train to the city every day.
Sometimes you would fall asleep and miss your stop.
Remember when you got fired
when you forgot to tell your boss we were going on vacation? You once
tried to paint my jeans black
because you put bleach in the wash by mistake.
There were so many mistakes I was not even aware of.
But deep inside I believed I was wearing you down with my lack of effort.
I did not help out enough around the house.
You stroked out because of ME!
You died of a broken heart because I failed
to live up to what a good son was supposed to be.
But Dad, I know now that I did not stop your heart from beating.
An illness did.
Let me shout out to the world. I AM NOT GUILTY!"

The poem is strong enough to make the evil Blue Ghoul disappear; more
evidence that his rules are a false message. The magicians watch the black
cloud of guilt lift off Rob's shoulders and slowly dissipate into the air. Rob
stands straighter than he ever has in his whole life.

COMMENTARY
CHAPTER ELEVEN - *THE GUILT POEM*

MAJOR CHARACTERS
Rob's Mother played by herself
Rob's Sister played by herself
Skin Divers played by themselves
Family near the Cave played by themselves
The Magicians, played by themselves
Blue Ghoul played by himself
Phantom played by himself
King and Queen played by themselves

Ever since my father's death, I had believed I was somehow responsible,
even though I was not always aware of these feelings. I started this "magical

99

thinking," as a teenager. It protected me against the complete powerlessness that trauma can bring, and also served to keep me from having to face the pain of my father's death. But this defense created as many problems as it solved.

I, like many other teens who have been traumatized, responded by acting out or withdrawing. If someone had told me I was not responsible, it might have helped. Probably the message would have needed many, many repetitions to sink in.

.In the narrative, guilt has taken over Rob's inner life. A whole set of demons were born of his guilt feelings, and they attacked him relentlessly. Gradually, he learns to face them. The first demon he meets is the Wicked Witch, who played the part of Supreme Guilt. She stated a recurring theme, that it was my fault that my father died. I had had these thoughts and feelings inside for years, but not until my work in the sandtray did I truly face my guilt feelings. The Wicked Witch says that Rob's laziness caused his father's energy to burn out, and consequently he got sick and died. The Witch chastises Rob for not crying at the funeral, for not even having the sense to fake tears. Rob also feels guilty about not knowing how or if he should comfort his mother and sister.

The Wicked Witch plays guilt again in the third tray. She yells at Rob for not grieving properly. She is angry because he never cried, never displayed remorse. She is enraged that he never helped his sister or mother with their pain.

During the fifth tray, the Rob learns that his father's death was caused by an illness, not him. For the first time, the belief that he killed his father is refuted. Up until this time, the Wicked Witch and the Grim Reaper have screamed derogatory, humiliating insults at the Rob while he has accepted their words as truth. Rob is still conflicted, however, as to how much guilt he really bears. He has a lot of work still to do.

In the succeeding trays, Rob partakes in rituals to initiate forgiveness, and does a lot of soul-searching. He is able to let go of some of his false responsibility for his father's death. Guilt moves over and allows a touch of forgiveness to enter.

In the tenth tray, though, Rob is still filled with guilt. He interprets the mother's face and body language as blaming the teenager for all that goes wrong, including his father's death. Note that this message comes from his mother's face and body language only. No words were stated. Rob thinks that if he could have only foreseen that his father was going to die, he could have comforted his mother and sister. The Wicked Witch tells Rob that he is the cause of all his family's misery, and if he feels guilty, he should. Finally, Rob's anger gives him the courage to stand up to all these voices of guilt, and he buries them all. This sets the scene for the eleventh tray, in which he writes a poem, a declaration to the world that he is not guilty of killing his father. You can feel the anger in the poem. Anger is not a "nice" emotion. The poem contains a lot of harsh criticism of my father, but writing and reading it really helped me find the strength to face his death and let go.

FAMILY DISCUSSION QUESTIONS
For Chapter Eleven - *THE GUILT POEM*

1.   Rob has difficulty sleeping in the beginning of this chapter. Do you ever have problems falling asleep? Do you ever wake up in the middle of the night and discover that you cannot fall asleep?

2.   Rob faces the one-year anniversary date of his father's death. Are anniversary dates important to you? Why?

3.   Rob talks about a dark cloud hovering over him. Have you ever felt like this?

4.   Rob picks up non-verbal cues from his mother and sister. What is your experience in picking up non-verbal cues? Have your perceptions ever turned out to be inaccurate?

5.   Rob has mixed feelings towards his mother. Talk about mixed feelings you have had.

6.   Do you ever look at family photos and experience numbness? What other feelings do you have?

7.   Rob reads a poem in this chapter titled *I Am Not Guilty*. Have you ever felt guilty about anything? Do you still feel that way? What other feelings and thoughts go with it? What do you do about it?

CHAPTER TWELVE

THE EVIL UPHEAVAL

THE EVIL UPHEAVAL

CHAPTER TWELVE

THE EVIL UPHEAVAL

Rob revs up the compact blue car and heads for route 18, bound for the shore. He has one foot through the floor on the gas pedal and the other foot is pounding out a beat from the radio. I can't get no satisfaction, indeed. Both hands are gripping the steering wheel in a vice lock. He is oblivious to the small cities that he drives through. All these towns butting up against each other like some cheap room dividers. He feels an anger building from the pit of his stomach to the top of his head. He wants to explode. He travels a lonely journey not only today, but every waking moment.

Even when he is with his friends, isolation is his frigid companion. When he is alone, he is frightened. When he is with friends, he would rather be alone. Nothing works very well. He thinks that with all he has been through, the demons he has faced, the time that has gone by and the guilt he has thrown off, he should feel better. Sometimes he does, but most days, like today, he is still miserable.

The temperature begins to cool down on this late summer afternoon. He hears the sound of the waves hitting the sand before he actually sees the pale salt water of the Jersey shore. Most people have left for the day after hours of trying to get as dark as the black people they despise and fear. Others are lazily walking on the boardwalk stuffing their faces with cotton candy and sausage sandwiches. He hears the noise from the arcades and the tinkling music coming from the carousel makes him downright exhausted.

He walks on the beach and stares at the people remaining there. There was a thunderstorm last evening that left a deep stream of water dividing up the beach in two sections. On the right side of the stream is a boisterous woman who is carrying on loudly while drinking a large glass of wine. She is standing next to a blue horse who gallops alongside.

Rob cannot believe his eyes –The Blue Ghoul, The Wicked Witch and Hitler have come on shore. Hitler, the mass murderer, the one who killed six million Jews, the icon of all that is evil in the world is here. Why is he here? What is going to happen? Rob wonders what evil deed he committed that warrants the entrance of Adolf Hitler. A man, woman and child playing happily together nearby seem oblivious to the darkness fifty yards away. A late afternoon runner slowly jogs past them, alone with the pleasant aura of intense exercise.

On the other side of the stream is his father's casket. Rob's father's coffin seems to follow him all over New Jersey, so he is not surprised to see it. Seeing his mother and sister in front of the grave is startling. The casket is buried in the sand. Three quarters of the coffin lid is uncovered. There are flowers on the casket surrounded by two majestic bright colored trees.

Rob finds the nerve to look at Hitler. He is drawn to Hitler out of fear of what treacherous act he will commit next. He also wonders, what forces in life create a monster like this? Hitler, his swastika hideously displayed as a crude, arrogant armband, wears his thick sickening mustache designed to hide the smile on his face each time he kills one of us. He murders without thought and he has no remorse, no conscience.

Rob feels hatred build up inside as he runs towards Hitler without any idea of what is supposed to transpire. He catches The Dictator off guard and manages to pick him up over his head and toss him like an old piece of meat into the ocean. Rob is totally out of breath and for a quick moment, relieved. He then stares at the part of the beach where Hitler had been. He feels no joy or resolve, only emptiness.

Rob is confused and dumfounded. He says to himself, "I just beat up and got rid of the most disreputable man in the history of the world. Shouldn't I be elated? Shouldn't I be proud? Why is hollowness all that I feel? Why do I feel numb and dead inside?

Out of desperation, Rob walks into the ocean, battles the waves, finds the disoriented Hitler and drags him back on the beach. Rob paces back and forth as he feels the rage build once again. He says, "I must eradicate all evil from the world!" This must be the purpose I was placed here on earth. Wiping out evil is my calling!"

His rage leads to digging up the sand with his bare hands. He grunts, sweats and his hands bleed. He knows no fear at this moment as he grabs Hitler by the lapels on his Nazi uniform and pushes him into a deep hole. He repeats this process with the Blue Ghoul and Wicked Witch. They do not resist because they are too stunned to react to Rob's fierceness.

All noise from the boardwalk and the ocean waves suddenly stops. All Rob can hear is his own breathing. He gets down on his hands and knees and prays that he will receive a sign from somewhere that he did the right thing. He is waiting for a sign that this action of burying the evil will banish the demons forever. He looks to the outside world to grace him with the message that he has destroyed evil forever and all time.

"Please, I ask that someone greater than myself bless this act. Please, I need you. I feel so lost, confused and frightened. I feel betrayed by my own universe," yells Rob to a deadly silence. He hopes that the act of burying evil will lead to the ultimate triumph where mayors have ticker tape parades and he gets to sit in the back seat of a convertible and wave to all the citizens who now love him.

He looks at the beach, and it is like half of the entire world has been buried. The earth is disheveled as if a warhead just exploded there. Something is definitely missing. This is not right. This is not the way. They are buried, but he still feels their presence. The burying is a desperate attempt to deny their existence. He allows himself to be with the scene in front of him. The bombed out earth, the buried, unmarked graves of the demons move him to sadness. He is surprised that he feels sad that the demons have vanished. In his wildest dreams, he did not imagine that he would ever react in this manner.

He finds a shovel and begins unburying the demons and wipes off the sand from their bodies. The removal of Hitler from the shoreline did not have the desired effect. The burying was even less successful. Hitler, The Blue Ghoul and the Wicked Witch cross over the stream of water and join the others at Rob's father's coffin. More demons and Rob meet them at the grave.

The evil ones in unison walk up to the others and pair up. They line up face to face. What is going to happen now? A nuclear explosion? A war to end all wars? The line up is now in progress and Rob feels powerless to thwart it. He fears that a blood-letting is now going to occur - a massacre so brutal that nothing will be left standing.

The wicked witch faces his sister and stares into her frightened eyes. The Silver Witch with the Raven on her arm faces his mother. Rob briefly looks at these pairings, but finds that he is unable to focus on them.

He takes a deep breath and watches the pairs have free rein. He chooses not to exercise control over them. They face each other, move closer then walk away. They eventually end up in close proximity, face to face.

Mr. Tuxedo, suave, altruistic, well loved for his generosity, is paired up with the Blue Ghoul. They are standing eyeball to eyeball. Violence is in the air and uncertainty rules the hour. Tuxedo exudes the confidence that Rob wishes he could possess. His hands are resting at his sides and his tux is clean and well pressed.

The Blue Ghoul is the guilt messenger. The guilt oozes out of his pores. He has no internal power to thwart the guilt running out of his body. He is guilty of not living up to the dreams and aspirations his parents have for him. Mr. Tuxedo, although much shorter than the Blue Ghoul, is ready to deal with him. Rob predicts that Mr. Tuxedo and the Ghoul will either physically fight or one of them will run away and withdraw.

Neither scene takes place today. Rob turns away, and then revisits the Mr. Tuxedo-Blue ghoul combination. The anger and hostility lifts. Somehow they are both aware at this exact moment that they can actually help each other. Blue Ghoul's guilt gives him compassion for others, which he can lend to Mr. Tuxedo. Mr. Tuxedo can pass along his good health, initiative and goodness to the Ghoul. There is a positive energy flowing between them now. Rob can almost see it.

He finds himself suddenly facing Hitler. Hitler is overwhelming, genocidal power. Rob is fearful and defenseless. Hitler says, "You are weak and useless; you must be destroyed like a stray animal." Rob replies, "Your evil penetrates my soul. I can do nothing to prevent you from killing me." Rob, while frightened beyond belief, stares into Hitler's face. Hitler has his right hand raised in the nazi salute, inches from the teenager's nose. He senses that blood shed is about to transpire. Rob foresees Hitler smashing his body into bits.

However, the expected confrontation never is initiated. Rob is able to observe his meeting with Hitler. He is able to rise above them and watch. The

107

rage dissipates. The fear dies out on the vine. Hitler brings power to Rob's helplessness, and Rob brings innocence, an open heart and meaning to Hitler. Hitler's arm drops. The Teenager, Rob stands strong.

While this drama was unfolding, the casket is totally covered with earth. The grave does not matter now. What has meaning is the coming together of the good and evil.

COMMENTARY
CHAPTER TWELVE - *THE EVIL UPHEAVAL*

MAJOR CHARACTERS
Adolf Hitler played by himself
Blue Ghoul played by himself
Wicked Witch played by herself
Mr. Tuxedo played by himself

I discovered another means of facing the demons. I had the good and evil figures pair up and face each other. They actually communicated. So far, I had managed to keep good and evil in separate compartments. I hadn't acknowledged that the evil figures, and the good ones came from within and were part of me. Today they met me and talked. They realized how they complemented each other. Then they began to integrate, to come together, to help each other. As it proceeded in further sandtrays, this integration enabled me to grow emotionally and spiritually.

I was able to experience this meeting and integration with the masculine figures. But for some reason, I was not ready to have this experience with the feminine characters. I was able to pair my sister and mother up with their own demons, but was not able to go any further with this process.

I had an empty and disconcerting experience when I removed and buried the demons. My teacher encouraged me to play with these figures. That involved unburying them, pairing them up and moving them in different configurations.

As I mentioned earlier, previous to my work in the sand, I had no healthy means to deal with the evil inside. My main defense was denial. Denial blocked

108

the pain from my consciousness, but also kept me from experiencing the richness of life. Through my work in the sand, I was learning alternatives for dealing with the demons.

One way was to identify the demons and calmly walk away. The second was to angrily bury them. At this point, however, these approaches were no longer effective. I realized I now had to face them and deal with them.. I had walked away from their hideousness. I had buried them in a blind rage. This work prepared me to face the evil and work with it for a long period of time.

My psyche had taught me how to tolerate the evil. I now knew that, if it became too overwhelming, I could walk away or bury it. I may feel sad, but I would be safe. Knowing that I could protect myself from the demons, that I could establish boundaries to keep them out, was new. It gave me the courage to engage the evil within instead of deny its existence.

FAMILY DISCUSSION QUESTIONS
For Chapter Twelve - *THE EVIL UPHEAVAL*

1.   Rob talks about the suburbs of New York City. Do you live in the city, suburbs or countryside? Talk about the pros and cons of your community.
2.   Rob witnesses white people attempting to get as dark as possible while sunning at the Jersey shore. Meanwhile these same people hate African Americans. Talk about your experiences with racism.
3.   Rob meets Adolf Hitler in this chapter. Talk about Hitler, genocide and hatred.
4.   Rob fights evil in this chapter. Do you believe in the existence of evil? Do you believe in God?
5.   The evil and good figures line up as dyads and face each other in this chapter. How do you feel about what transpired here?
6.   Do you believe you have "good" and "bad" sides to you? If so, how do you feel about the "bad" parts? Do you believe these different parts of you can work together?

CHAPTER THIRTEEN

WHEN FORGIVENESS ENTERS

CHAPTER THIRTEEN CONTINUED

WHEN FORGIVENESS ENTERS

CHAPTER THIRTEEN

WHEN FORGIVENESS ENTERS

Robins and blue jays chirping outside his bedroom window awaken Rob. He wonders when was the last time he was aware of the birds' morning singing. The brightness of the sun warms up his face. He sticks his head outside the window and surveys his back yard. His father's coffin is in the center with tropical flowers, lush, bright colored trees and green moss encircling it. He is neither perplexed nor frustrated at this discovery. Matter of fact, he welcomes the opportunity to face his father's casket again. He picks a bunch of red berries out of the garden and places them on the grave and smiles. His smiles contain the wisdom that grief is ongoing, and its terrible pain can be healed.

It is such a clear day that he can see the river and park from his house. He senses that the demons are lurking about somewhere. His visits to his father's grave have taught him many things. One of them is that the demons are never far away. He gazes at the river and, lo and behold, on the shore stands a whole pack of them lined up side to side. Rob gets aquatinted with them one by one. A brown winged Pegasus screams out in rage. The Wicked Witch taunts all that dare to get close to her. The Gremlin is terrifying and his breath would melt the world's most indestructible metal. There is a large tiger whose stripes boldly announce the animal's fierceness, ready to pounce on any perceived enemy.

The Wizard does not look dangerous, although Rob senses the Wizard's stance is deceptive. He looks into his crystal and plots strategy leading to mass destruction. The Giant White Bear prowls into view. He has the deadly combination of brute strength, graceful agility and burning speed in his arsenal. He serves to keep the other demons in check.

Rob feels no need to run away, although he is aware that he can move out swiftly if he needs to. He is shocked that he is not afraid of the demons. Now he is keeping his distance from them, but the acute fear that captured him in the past is not present. He does not know why he is not afraid, but does not judge his feelings. He trusts that his journey will further enlighten him. He takes several deep breaths to relax and is not surprised to see creatures that are nurturing and pleasant standing across the river on the opposite shore.

A playful dolphin keeps jumping out of the water, splashing with wild abandon. Rob finds himself over on the pleasant creatures' side of the river. His arms and legs feel loose and easy. His neck is not stiff and the rest of his body is pain free. "When is the last time I felt like this?" he shouts out to the world. A naked baby stands near Rob. He says, "This baby is me. He is all of my innocence that was taken away when my father died. Will innocence ever return"?

From the corner of his left eye, The Mermaid swims confidently upstream. She is protecting the baby's innocence. She is playful like the dolphin, strong like the bear and fierce like the tiger. She brings a sense of peace to all that touch her presence.

Meanwhile in the middle of the river, The Blue Ghoul raises his ugly head and walks into the shallow part of the water.

He walks all over the river and he is able to keep afloat even in the river's deepest regions. From his current vantage point, he can see the entire town. He turns around to face the others and stares into Rob's blue eyes. Rob does not flinch, and he is not afraid. The Blue Ghoul's stare radiates heat on Rob's pupils, but he does not turn away. Rob knows that it is time to face the Ghoul on his newly discovered terms.

He says, "I know that for some reason you are supposed to be here. Life is filled with both good and evil. I cannot make you perish, nor at this time is that my desire. It is my quest to someday understand your purpose. You feel like you are a part of me that I can neither divorce or kill."

Rob now feels that all that he sees, feels and hears is part of him. The Silly Flute Man walking across the river is one example. The music, light and airy flows inside and outside him. He is having fun by himself and does not need anyone else at this moment. He hopes that the others enjoy his sound, but is not overly concerned if they are indifferent.

A multi-hued Peacock hovers over the water and is face to face with the Blue Ghoul. They are polar opposites that somehow know that they need each other in order for the world to exist. The Peacock is not afraid of the Ghoul, and the Ghoul, in turn does not want to devour the beautiful bird.

Of course the day would not be complete without guilt, and here comes Mr. Guilt himself. He joins the row of demons and raises the ax above the horns implanted in his head. His huge teeth are bared in a gruesome manner. Mr. Guilt will not be waylaid from the task at hand. His job is to shake the confident foundations of all he comes to meet. He does not believe that anyone has the right to be guilt free.

The Turquoise Horse stands to the right of the silly flute guy. The Horse is dignified beauty. He can protect and ride like the wind. He is dependable and honorable. The Maiden in the light blue dress is placed next to the horse. She is kindness. Her right arm is extended in an effort to reach out to those in pain. She is soothing.

St. Martin is placed to the right of the maiden. He is the quiet wisdom that lives in this world. He is wearing a black robe that hangs to his feet. He never frets or worries. Rob knows that he can ask him questions if the need arises. A Fireman holding a child in his left arm is placed to the right of St. Martin. The Fireman has just rescued the child from a burning building. The child is bewildered, but safe. The Fireman is a hero.

There are heroes and demons, wise and kind ones in the world today. The demons do not frighten so much. The good ones do not create excess excitement. They all just are.

A stone bridge is placed connecting one shore of the river to the other. Rob hears a sudden thud, and then serenity washes over him. Suddenly, stones that are red, green, clear and orange are placed on the bridge and in the river. They are gravestones celebrating life, grieving death and celebrating life again. The stones are the cycle we all live in. Large, pretty flowers are floating in the river. They honor all the pain, misery, hope, fear and love Rob has lived. The flowers honor all Rob's life experiences.

The world is alive and more of its nature enters. A Walrus is placed behind the Wizard with the cane. He is playful and childlike. A light amber butterfly with brown edges slowly glides until she lands in front of the baby. Mr. Party Man is placed behind the teenager. He raises a glass of wine and offers a toast. He says, "Let us drink to all the suffering and joy before us today." He drinks the red wine with robust pleasure.

Tears begin to well up in Rob's eyes as he begins a speech. "Yes Party Man, I have suffered from pain, numbness and plain old misunderstanding. It is so sad that I did not have the capabilities to deal with the death of my father. This led me to so many closed doors and the belief that all was futile. This must be what forgiveness is, to honor and let go of all the hurt inside. Let us commence with a forgiveness ceremony"

The Peacock begins this service by slowly opening his plume. The blue, yellow and green feathers come slowly into view as the sunlight pours down between them. Rob feels as though he is embracing himself inside. He is sad, happy, and grateful all at once. He says, "Forgiveness has unlocked my spirit. I am no longer rigid and am beginning to see alternatives for experiencing good and evil. Their different forces cannot wipe each other out. I used to believe that good needed to destroy evil in the world in order to create peace. I now know that this is impossible. I forgive myself for living with this belief for so long. Good, evil, and even guilt are different aspects of life. This is a belief to be embraced, not fought against. When forgiveness enters, all life can coexist.

COMMENTARY
CHAPTER THIRTEEN - *WHEN FORGIVENESS ENTERS*

MAJOR CHARACTERS
Brown Winged Pegasus played by himself
Supreme Guilt played by the Wicked Witch
The Gremlin played by himself
Tiger played by himself
Wizard played by himself
Giant White Bear played by himself
Dolphin played by himself
Baby played by himself
Mermaid played by herself
Blue Ghoul played by himself
Peacock played by himself
Mr. Guilt played by himself
St. Martin De Porres played by himself
Fireman holding child played by themselves

Mr. Party Man played by himself

I learned more about forgiveness in today's tray. Forgiveness heals the split that guilt can create. I continued to experiment with matching good and evil figures, building different alignments and structures. I experienced the freedom of moving figures around; no longer having the mindset that life had to be stagnant. In fact, life could not stand still, and never can. I was learning that good and evil are elements that cannot be eliminated. They exist inside all of us.

When I started to forgive myself and integrate the different parts of me, and the different parts of life, I was able to begin to let go of my father. I started to forgive myself for my actions, beliefs and feelings around his death, most of which hurt nobody except me. Up to this point, my father's casket was placed in every tray. It took all these visits to begin to let go.

In #1, I met my father's casket for the first time. This was part of the initial step of breaking through the denial of his death. Rob witnessed the workman unceremoniously throwing dirt on the casket. This sandtray brought back my funeral memories. I discovered that this was the moment my internal numbness was born.

In #2, the casket is the first figure placed in the tray. It is described as a rusty metal coffin. It is no longer a hazy image pushed into the recesses of my memory bank. It has a definitive shape and look about it. It is in the center, all alone. I took in the numbing effect of the casket, the emptiness that death can bring, by experiencing it without any other distractions. . An electrified fence was placed around the casket. I learned that this fence was society's rules that prevented me from facing my father's death.

In # 3, the casket returns to the center of the tray. I stated that it was difficult to visualize my father in the coffin. This was the first time I considered burying the coffin. At the time of this tray, I did not realize the significance of burying the casket. I would learn later what this act would mean.

However, I did not bury the casket in this tray. I did discover the bridge, which was a gateway between life and death. The land of death held the coffin and the hole, while the land of life had beauty and a castle full of dreams. This was how I first began to understand that I had choices in dealing with my feelings.

116

In # 4, the casket was placed in the center of a bridge. It was now off the ground, forcing all to look up at it instead of focusing downward. This placement indicates my newly found ability to celebrate my father's life and death.

The raising of the casket opened up memory chambers that have been locked up for twenty-five years. A ghost stands on top of the casket. The ghost is my dead father. Experiencing this ghost allowed me to further celebrate his life and death. I learned that my father gave me his strengths. I did not obtain them all by myself.

In #5, the casket is again in the center of the world. This sandtray enabled me to actually experience that he was really dead, that he is never coming back. I was no longer frightened of this truth. I stopped denying that he really died.

A Wizard stood on the casket. He asked all those present have a moment of silence to recognize the life and death of my father. I buried my father's casket and cried. The tears that had been thwarted by numbness in the past flowed from my eyes onto my shirt. The tears helped make his death real. Without tears, there is no real sadness, and mourning is not possible.

Tears opened the way for grief to proceed. In #7, I buried the casket in the center of the sandtray. I smoothed sand on the top of it. I created the funeral in the manner I would have liked it to be. I asked, "Why did he have to die, Why did he leave me?" I cried deeply. The headstone is transformed into a quartz heart. I lay flowers on the grave for the first time. I took in all the sadness that the flowers brought. I have largely accepted the finality of his death.

In #8, the casket is placed on top of the grave. I felt no need to bury it. I placed flowers all around the coffin. This tray took in elements of the last few sandtrays. I combined the funeral service, the memorial and honoring my father's life. I celebrated his life and mourned his loss. I noticed that the absence of guilt allows grieving to occur.

In #9, the casket is placed on a mountaintop, even more out in the open, indicating my deeper acceptance of his death. In # 10, the casket is originally placed on top of a hill. All the demons, which are the myths of how to deal with death, were buried. I stood alone with my father's casket. These myths were now refuted. They had previously blocked the path to face his death. I was now able to take that path without fear, without guilt.

In #11, flowers are placed around the casket. The flowers honor the hope that I can talk about my father's loss with my mother. This is the first time I talked about the possibility of having a dialogue with any family member about his death. In # 12, a lot of action took place while the casket was buried. The casket, for the first time was not the central focus of the world. The coming together of good and evil was. In 13a, I placed the casket in the center of the world, almost completely covered it with sand and embellished it with flowers, trees, and moss. I placed a branch of red berries across the grave, and then I smiled. I walked away to begin building a new world.

I experienced a sense of completion of this portion of the journey, breaking through the denial of death, but there was a long journey ahead and more demons to face.

FAMILY DISCUSSION QUESTIONS
For Chapter Thirteen - *WHEN FORGIVENESS ENTERS*

1.   The changes in seasons are significant to Rob. How does the changing of the seasons affect you?
2.   Rob realizes that the internal demons are always lurking about? Do you agree?
3.   Rob feels that all his innocence was taken away when his father died. How do you feel about innocence?
4.   Rob realizes that life is filled with both good and evil. Do you agree?
5.   Rob experiences a fireman as a hero in this chapter. Do you have any heroes or heroines?
6.   Rob has a forgiveness ceremony in this chapter. Talk about forgiveness. Has anyone ever forgiven you? Have you forgiven other? How did forgiving or being forgiven make you feel?
7.   What do you think has to happen for forgiveness to occur?

CHAPTER FOURTEEN

PUSHING AWAY LOVE

CHAPTER FOURTEEN

PUSHING AWAY LOVE

Rob finds himself standing in front of a blue and gray castle that is enshrouded in fog. The castle looks comfortable, warm and inviting and he wonders what it is like inside. He looks down the street and he realizes that he is unfamiliar territory. He does not know where he is and has no idea how he got here, but he is not worried. He looks down the road and is taken in by the sight of a huge pyramid. He takes a deep breath and appreciates his calm state of being.

The pyramid is ancient and mesmerizing. It provides a holding place for the sacred. Rob is astounded that his mind came up with this description, but he does not judge himself. Nothing can penetrate the walls of the centuries old structure. Rob feels its history and glory radiate through his being. He notices that he is not thinking or dwelling about his life problems. He is focusing on what is happening in front of him.

"What a beautiful tree", Rob yells out to no one in particular. He is so excited that he is talking out loud to himself. "You should see this tree, it is unbelievable! I have never seen anything like it before. It is a large tree that takes up three city blocks and its leaves are made of gold!"

The light from the moon is reflecting on the golden leaves and causing them to twinkle. Rob feels a twinge of fear jolt him out of his mesmerized state and into the linear caverns of his mind. His thoughts are not introspective. They are the jittery sound bites of panic. He ponders: What is the meaning of the Golden Tree? How does it fit into his life? Is this tree going to be a positive or negative experience? What is going to happen after he experiences the Golden Tree? He feels his stomach doing somersaults and his neck tightening up like a stretched out piece of rubber.

"What in the hell just happened? One minute I was enjoying the sparkling leaves of the Golden Tree and the next minute I was analyzing what I was feeling, breathing, seeing and hearing. Why do I do that? I always do this. I cannot seem to leave the joyful present moment alone without falling back to analyzing, reviewing, and categorizing the experience."

Rob rubs his face and notices facial hair growing above his lip. He is so confused about what is the right way to live. "Should I just let things be or should I try to figure out the why, who, where, what for of every snap shot of life that comes?"

OK. He knows that he will not find the answer to this dilemma by hitting thoughts around his brain like a ping-pong ball lost in orbit. He never finds answers to his problems this way – only temporary stopgaps that lower the fear intensity for a minute or less. Then it is back to the "you have to understand the sum total of the experience before you can relax and enjoy it" routine.

He knows the Golden Tree holds the answer, so he lifts his head and returns his focus to the reflecting leaves and the majestic trunk. The glittering leaves move in and out of shadows and light. The leaves are brighter than the stars in the sky. He pays attention to his body and not his head. This is a novel concept. Every time he sees a leaf glimmer, his heart becomes full, warm and achy with happiness for being alive. He is so lucky to be alive and witness the tree. He suddenly feels the terrible jolt of fear tremble up and down his spine.

"Now wait", he actually holds up his hand in an effort to stop the adrenaline rush of panic that now occupies his stomach, neck, and shoulders. Instead of going to the analyzing mode that he has habitually done in this kind of situation all his life, he returns his attention to the tree. He says, "I do not have to figure if the tree has a hidden meaning. There is no hidden meaning waiting to trap me in its clutches. This tree is not an object to guard against! Rob is so relieved to learn that he does not have to laboriously search every wonderful moment for dreadful covert meanings. He does not diminish this euphoria by searching for hidden dangers.

Rob walks around some more and continues to reflect, "Why have I always had this painful method of being with happy times?" He looks at the blinking light reflected off the leaves, like fireflies in the darkness, and the response comes to him as strong as truth can be told. He searches for hidden uncertainties and concealed dangers in an effort to gain control over his life, the world, what happens next, everything.

"OK. So how has this way of living operated? What price have I paid for being so vigilant?" He returns his energy to the golden tree. Its creativity, beauty and uniqueness fascinate him. Then fear comes up in the distant regions

121

of his being and then quickly this anxiety takes over the core of his being. He then asks himself, "Why am I fascinated by this glittering tree? What is it about the tree that makes me feel so at ease?

This self-interrogation takes him right back to his head and the analyzing mode. He has come to believe that being fascinated by life is not enough. Rob is obsessed with knowing what is behind anything he experiences. He needs to know why he likes that golden tree so much.

He has believed that behind every experience is a guiding force made up of systematic definitions. He considers them insights, but in reality they are only words that hold no meaning because they are not connected to any memory, feeling, or experiences. He is learning now that this belief system is filled with falsehoods. This searching is not expanding the experience; it is blocking and constricting it.

Puck is dressed in clothes that seem centuries old. He is a joker, a funnyman who appears as a child. Rob starts analyzing Puck, his clothes and his posture. Puck has his hand out and Rob wonders if he is panhandling for coins. If he is begging, Rob wonders, "why am I focusing on such a desperate character? Is it because he reminds me of myself? Is it because I am afraid of him? Is it because he is getting ready to attack me?"

Rob realizes he is pondering all this worry in his brain. He leaps out of his head. He pays attention to his body. He listens to his breathing. He experiences warmth around his face and ears. He looks at Puck. He moves away from the analyzer inside. Puck is a little kid. He is innocence. He has his hand out asking for money to go to the store to buy candy. Puck's innocence and child-like qualities are touching. He is sad at the loss of his own innocence.

The attempt to master complete comprehension of every life scenario is based on a fear response. Rob has to know everything about Puck, about the Golden Tree, about every facet of life in order to feel secure. If Rob does not feel secure, then somehow this beauty can harm him.

He looks again at the Golden Tree. He says," because I am afraid, I cannot trust the beauty. I worry that there is something behind it; afraid to face whatever it is on a feeling level. Maybe there is a tornado behind that tree. Maybe that tree is going to die someday. If the tree dies, I will be lost the way I was when my father died. You have to prepare yourself."

However Rob knows that there is no lesson in life that prepares us for dealing with death. He has learned this truth by hard experience. One cannot anticipate what feelings, hurts, and emotional roller coasters will transpire in the future. Rob knows now that it is impossible to predict and manage what feelings will arise when trauma strikes.

Infinity enters next. He is placed in the bottom center of the world. Infinity is a silver snake who is eating himself. Infinity, like life, is endless. Rob begins an analysis once more. He thinks, "All this stuff about staying on top of it, figuring it out, being prepared is a tragic waste of time. It is a futile attempt to put a halt to the endless cycle of life."

"This is a method used to guard, used to protect. It is a disconnected process that takes me out of the present. This process takes me out of my body, heart and spirit. Life just is. I cannot change that by doing all this watching out."

Goodness exists as evil does. The struggle of holding the good is similar to the difficulty of holding the evil. When Rob buries the demons or throws them out of the tray, their power still remains. They are only dealt with when finally faced and talked to. On the other hand, when goodness initially comes forth, Rob experiences a short burst of euphoria and excitement. Then he gets frightened and asks, "Why is this so great?" It gets intellectualized away.

Rob suddenly finds himself standing on skis next to his father who is likewise on skis. The Skiers are together and they are enjoying each other's company, just having fun. Rob remembers joyful memories of his father and him having fun. He mulls this over, "So alright, I think I understand the nature of evil, but what about the goodness that is also part of life?" Living with the goodness is as difficult to accept as facing the evil demons.

Rob's core system was somehow trained to believe that if something positive happens, an intense traumatic event will follow, or the good event will be stripped away. If he allows himself to fully experience the Skiers as his father and himself, he is afraid it will lead to a terrifying conclusion. Rob's eyes tear up when he realizes how much he misses his father and how much of the goodness of life he has lost over the years, how much love he has pushed away.

123

If someone is nice to him, anxiety kicks into high gear. He questions why someone would be nice to him. What has he done to deserve respectful treatment? How does he reciprocate? What price does Rob have to pay in order to be loved? He is so sad now. He says," If someone does something nice for me, I cannot trust it because it will never stay. It will leave just like my father did. I try to cling to the niceness by attempting to figure out a way to keep it. Keep it so it is safe, not a threat." Rob tries to create love in his life, then pushes it away through numbness, depression, and intellectualization.

The brightly hued Peacock proudly raises his feathers of blue, green and gold. The Peacock is forgiveness. In the Peacock's presence, Rob can forgive himself for carrying the huge burden of deep worry. He feels its rigid intensity leave his body.

He attempts to understand forgiveness better. Understanding why someone has hurt him leads to forgiveness. Understanding comes from the willingness to walk in the other person's shoes, to empathize with that person. That willingness begins when Rob no longer wants to carry the burden of hatred.

Without the ability to empathize, you cannot forgive yourself or others. You cannot forgive unless you can understand, and you cannot understand if you cannot feel. If you cannot feel anything, then you are lost. You cannot grieve. You cannot understand, and you cannot forgive. All you will get is the numbness. You cannot see the beauty and you cannot see the truth.

The Light Bearer who walks nearby gives Rob direction. It is so easy to get lost. Rob is aware that he has felt lost over and over again. There are so many ways to get lost when you do not let yourself feel your truth.

A father, mother and son are playing near the golden tree. They are oblivious to the problems of the world around them. They receive energy from each other simply by caring. Mother and Father love the baby unconditionally. Baby knows that. He basks in the euphoria of being loved for who he is. The baby feels it and knows it, and he does not have to know the definition of love. He can go out into the world and have faith that whatever happens will work out.

Whatever crisis occurs, there will be light at the end of the tunnel. Rob is overcome with sadness at this juncture. He feels that he never got the richness of being loved unconditionally. He was not loved for who he was. Rob is aware that he has difficulty loving himself in this manner as well.

The Wizards, who are in the upper left of the world, are full of joy and having fun. They say in unison, "We are here. You may not think we are here, but you cannot get rid of us. You cannot banish us. You cannot cut out anything that ever happened in your life. You cannot dissolve traumatic experiences. They are here and you have to learn to live without bitterness. Bitterness is not in this world today because goodness has been allowed to enter. Bitterness comes from being stuck. Bitterness comes from not allowing the goodness to enter."

The Wizards tell Rob that they are not a threat to him. He feels his guard disappear, and he lights a candle. The Wizards can move from calmness to acceptance to euphoria. All those feelings are OK. They are not dangerous. He looks at the multi-colored trees. They form a forest. Once upon a time there was a force that taught him that he was not allowed to embrace the goodness. Now he knows that these feelings of goodness are not dangerous. They will not harm him.

COMMENTARY
CHAPTER FOURTEEN - *PUSHING AWAY LOVE*

MAJOR CHARACTERS
Golden Tree played by itself
Puck played by himself
Infinity played by himself
Loving Family played by Baby's First Steps
The Wizards played by themselves

I experienced the differences between thinking and feeling in this tray. Up to this point I had major difficulties in separating them. However, today's world was a mere introduction into this separation. As I read this entry, I saw myself allowing for short bursts of experiences and then returning to my intellectual self. I lived most of my life inside my head and nowhere else.

I realized that this analyzing mode was a defense designed to protect me from harm. I was at least as fearful of the good as I was the evil. The intense "figuring out" immediately takes me away from the experiencing realm. I had the belief system that being fascinated by life was not allowed. I needed to know the hidden dangers behind the fascination. This search was not introspection, but a myopic hypervigilance that knew no rest.

I was able to get out of my head in the scene when Puck enters. I paid attention to my body sensations and began to differentiate that process from merely thinking about it. I connected to what I was seeing. It was the difference between analyzing and experiencing. I began to live my experience and allowed Puck to come to life, as I allowed the demons come to life earlier.

I learned that I had to know all the details and makeup of all the figures in the tray, hence the entire world around me. I thought if I knew everything, then I would feel secure against danger. My belief system was that the world was a very dangerous place. This feeling of security was fiercely sought, but never attained because you can never know everything. Although I desperately believed this was the road to truth, it was not the path to inner peace.

This need for total, guaranteed security came from the trauma of my father's death. My father's death was a surprise attack on my psyche. This trauma led me to believe that life was to be spent warding off danger and insecurity, because life only brought danger and insecurity. This belief led me to the illusion that it was possible to protect myself from potential hardship by knowing exactly what was going to occur the next moment. Of course, this task was impossible and created huge worry and anxiety.

During my work in this tray, I learned that all this worrying, preparing, analyzing was a waste of time. This mode of living also kept me from experiencing the present. I was too worried about the future to feel, experience or hold on to any uplifting moments.

I had pushed evil away by burying and throwing its force out of the tray. I pushed love, that is, the power of goodness away by refusal to accept its existence. My lifestyle led me to react to the goodness instead of taking it in. I reacted by believing that the goodness was only a temporary facade that covered the evil. The layers of this complexity unveiled itself today. I was afraid that I did not deserve goodness and therefore would have to pay a steep price for receiving its benefits. Furthermore, I believed that life-threatening upheaval

126

would follow any acts of goodness. My personality developed into a rigid set of double binds that allowed little happiness or love to get through.

This tray taught me that I did not have to live like this anymore. I can now find beauty in the Golden Tree. I can hold it in my heart. I do not have to push it away. The beauty will make me feel whole and ultimately, secure.

I learned how to differentiate between experiencing, and analyzing and worrying. I had thought my only choices were experiencing fear, worry, etc. or not experiencing at all. My defense against experiencing evil was simply refusing to experience the world in front of me. I would be so frightened that there would be no sense in looking at anything.

An experience is living in the present moment without fear, worry, shame or anxiety. Facing where the fears come from is experiencing. To experience is to hold the joy, sadness or other feeling without the force that pushes it away. It is felt fully throughout my whole body. To analyze is to merely interface with the thinking mode. It takes place only in my head.

Worry is fear-based. It begins in my head then is felt as abrupt panic in different parts of my body, mostly the stomach. Thinking and worrying do not result in any sense of completion or well- being. These feelings come through experiencing. Discovering truth is part of the experiencing process. Discovering and understanding truth is what I want to explore in future worlds.

The ways we approach life in the sandtray are often the same ways we treat the outer world. I had several methods of pushing away the experiences in the sandtray world. I could simply not look at the world in front of me, or I could deny that experiences truly exist and believe that only thoughts exist. By hurrying to put words to the experience, I could take myself out of the world and into the narrow regions of the intellect. By focusing on why a scene is the way it is, instead of what it is, I tried to put distance between the experience and my feelings. These distancing moves were my effort to minimize the risk, based on my belief that all experiences are not only bad, but dangerous things that must be wiped away.

When I focus on what is in front of me, it widens the experience and opens up possibilities. I have outlined the kind of thoughts that interfere with experiencing. There is also thought that reflects on experiencing, that combines experiencing and thinking together. Reflection enhances experiencing. It

127

alternates thinking and experiencing until the point is reached where experiencing and reflecting unite as one.

FAMILY DISCUSSION QUESTIONS
For Chapter Fourteen - *PUSHING AWAY LOVE*

1.   Do you ever find yourself not paying attention to what is happening right in front of you? Talk about this kind of experience.
2.   Rob realizes that he tends to over analyze his experiences. He is moved by the beauty of the Golden Tree, but soon stops appreciating it and starts thinking about it instead. Do you have a tendency to do this as well?
3.   Rob learns that he has spent much of his life searching for hidden dangers. Do you dwell on looking for hidden dangers?
4.   Rob says that to forgive someone, you have to empathize, that is, "to walk in the other person's shoes." Do you try to empathize with others? What happens when you do?
5.   The Wizards tell Rob he should accept the goodness in life and not be afraid of it. Do you find it easy to accept positive experiences?
6.   Rob has an intense interaction with Puck in this chapter. In his anxiety, he saw Puck as a threat or a loser. When he stepped back and relaxed, he realized Puck was an innocent, adorable child. Have you ever had an experience like Robs? Like Puck's?
7.   Rob talks about insecurity during this chapter. What makes you feel insecure? What makes you feel secure?

CHAPTER FIFTEEN

CELEBRATION OF JOY

CHAPTER FIFTEEN

CELEBRATION OF JOY

Rob drives over to the park with the zoo, at the bottom of the suburbs. He has never liked seeing animals locked up in cages for the amusement of gawking humans. However, he does love the park's lush green open spaces and tall trees that hide the busy road just beyond the park's boundaries. His school attendance continues to be dismal at best. He has missed at least one class a day since his father died. Rob is so far behind in his studies that doing any homework at this point seems beyond futility.

The park is pretty empty because it is very late on a weekday afternoon. Although he had lunch at the sweet shop hours ago, he still has the sweet and greasy tastes of catsup, French fries, and burgers on his tongue. He is in a reflective mood as he walks around with his hands behind his back and his eyes looking at the ground.

He wishes that he had a different relationship with his mother and sister. He has such trouble connecting with them. He has a visual image of those two stuck in his mind, where they huddle in a corner of the room, deathly afraid of him, scared to death of his rage. He is filled with guilt when this picture flashes before his eyes. He does not remember what he did to terrify them so much. Maybe they were afraid of the angst, anger, and turmoil that he holds for all three of his family.

He thinks about his former girlfriend and he winces inside. She was so beautiful, and for some reason she wanted him. He could not believe his luck, and he pinched himself everyday to make sure he was not dreaming. He walked hand in hand with her through the halls of the high school, back in the days when he used to attend regularly. She had long brown hair and a smile that made him feel downright goofy. When she touched him, he could swear he was in heaven.

But that is all over now. She broke up with him shortly after his father died. She did not give him a reason when she returned his Four Tops albums and his ring. Sometime later he saw her walking down the street holding hands with his so- called best friend. Betrayal. The experience of betrayal, sticking like a knife wound in his ribs, was so awful. He cried alone for weeks.

He once believed that betrayal and death of a loved one would end any chance of further happiness. He used to believe that he would never recover from these hurts. Now he knows that he will.

There are bright colored trees throughout the park and their leaves are rich in shades of red, orange, yellow and brown. They are leaves of fall that will soon fall to the ground as winter approaches. Rob stares at the trees and takes in the cycle of life that the changing of the seasons echoes.

The red leaves celebrate birth and renewal, and the green ones are the day-to-day joy of living. The golden leaves that are beginning to float towards the ground are impending loss. Rob watches the leaves as they silently brush the ground and find a resting place in the grass. He is amazed to discover that this sense of loss is not traumatizing, or frightening. No guilt bells are going off. He gets down on his knees and bows his head as a way of accepting that loss is part of life. At this moment Rob's mind, spirit, body and heart are as one like planets in alignment. There is no question, no doubt that this new discovery is the truth. There is no need to fight this reality any longer.

Evening has come, bringing out the stars and moon, and Rob decides it is time for a party to celebrate the life all around him and within him. He goes to a pay phone to dial up musicians, dancers and other revelers. The Drummer with his pastel outfit is the first to show, and he takes the conga out of its bag and begins to beat out an Afro-Cuban rhythm. He is oblivious to his surroundings as he is into the sweet music coming off his hands. It pounds through his veins and pumps blood to his heart. He is part of a band and he is warming up awaiting his cohorts.

Glenda, the Pink Witch gracefully glides into the party with her wand in the air. She starts to get into the music and gets down to the beat of the drummer as she fluidly dances across the night grass with the moon reflecting on her wand. What a way to get a party started! She is smiling and Rob basks in her warm, protective and understanding light.

Neptune, the golden god of the sea asks Glenda to dance and she politely accepts. He carries a staff that serves as a walking stick and magic wand, like

131

Glenda. He does not have legs, only fins and the tail of a fish, but this does not hinder him on the dance floor. Rob watches Neptune tap his staff to the Drummer's rhythm and takes in his quiet strength and inner sense of well-being.

People from miles around have heard the first drumbeats and are flocking to this celebration. Most folks have no idea what the celebration is about, but there is magic in the air, smiles on faces and friendliness all around. Two Mexican guitar players strum along with the Afro-Cuban beat to create an intense, pounding yet gentle love.

A baby and his parents sit down in the middle of all the festivities. The baby is about two years old and he is standing between the two adults. His father's eyes are all aglow with love and acceptance as his mother reaches out to touch him with both hands and arms. The baby feels safe and loved for all time. Rob's initial warmth upon gazing at this scene turns into fear, confusion and sadness. He wonders if his parents ever touched him in this way. Just a microsecond would have been good enough, but he has no sense or memory of this total embrace.

This empty feeling is lifted when Puck walks up to Rob and begins telling silly jokes that cause him to laugh hysterically. Puck is playful, relaxed and so carefree that he does not have the time for troubles. He has wings that allow him to fly in and out of different planes of existence. He walks through many realms of the universe. Puck is childlike, innocent and alive. Rob misses the carefree childhood that he never had.

The drumming, singing and guitar playing continue as the man of the hour comes on the scene. The Silver Torch Carrier walks up to the band and points his fiery bright torch to the sky. It burns bright hues of orange, yellow and blue. He is a supreme guide who Rob immediately places his faith in. He is determined to lead Rob on his rough and tumble journey from numbness to the demons and beyond.

The Torch Carrier says, "I will show you the way and you can follow. As you know, this is not a smooth, steady, clear ride. No, your journey is filled with potholes, land mines, screaming witches, bats and devils. But it is also filled with bright colored trees, moon lit nights and people kinder than you ever imagined. Nature is part of life as well as obstacles are." Rob sits with this for a moment and replies, "I used to believe that life, a real man's life, was free of

132

obstacles. I used to believe that I created all these roadblocks myself. I now know that none of this is true."

Rob looks up at a Grandfather Clock and thinks that time is moving so quickly; that he needs to reach the end of his journey soon. He needs to find all the answers immediately. He continues to take in the ticking of the clock and realizes that his journey cannot be hurried along no matter how fast he wants it to go. It moves at its own pace and Rob simply has no control over it.

Rob looks out into the sky and sees a mirror image of Earth. This earth is spinning slowly on its axis, and he can see the colors of different countries, lakes, and oceans slowly turn. Rob notices that he feels part of the earth, and the familiar feeling of alienation disappears. His heart moves with each turn of the earth's eternal axis.

The town athlete, who is a gifted Runner, glides into the party. The sweat glistens from his forehead and soaks up his shirt. He has long blond hair that blows in the breeze and whenever he runs, he feels a sense of freedom few have experienced. He is free because he is not dependent on any one for direction or approval.

Rob joins the party and allows his emotions to run wild along with the Puerto Rican rhythm the drummer is pounding out. Suddenly tears come to his eyes unexpectedly. The Drummer's hands are now his hands. He feels the skin of the conga on his fingertips and palms. At the same time he feels his legs becoming stronger with each stride as he runs into the night. Rob cries out, "I am the Drummer, I am the Runner!" I am not death; I am neither the Rabbi nor the devil. I am not my father. I am Rob!

Rob loves to play music and he loves to have fun. He says, "Here comes my mother and dad. Listen how he plays the violin and harmonica. Listen to how she tries to accompany him on the piano. Watch as they gaze into each other's eyes, as they are lost in the sound of their music coming together. Boy, they really loved each other, didn't they?"

COMMENTARY
CHAPTER FIFTEEN - *CELEBRATION OF JOY*

MAJOR CHARACTERS
Glenda the Pink Witch played by herself
The Drummer played by himself
Neptune played by himself
Baby and his Parents played by themselves
Puck played by himself
Silver Torch Carrier played by himself
The Runner played by himself

The transition from the pre-teen years to being a teenager is difficult even in the best of situations. Adolescents' physical, emotional and spiritual states are in constant flux, leading to overwhelming confusion. One minute they desire independence, the next moment they want a significant adult in their lives to give them solutions to their problems. This is all part of normal development as teens seek to establish their own identities, separate and different from their parents.

My teenage identity search was derailed by my father's death. The normal tasks of teenage development were exacerbated by the trauma of his loss. My father died before I could attempt to "break away" from him. Therefore, with the dark cloud of his emotionally unresolved death always hovering over me, I saw myself primarily as a victim, a fatherless son, the boy who could not connect with the rest of his family, the kid with the bad grades, the loser with no future whatsoever.

During this tray, I was able to connect with the "new" Rob inside. My father's coffin was no longer the centerpiece of each sandtray. Now it was time to embrace the parts of myself that were either pushed away by denial or because I did not feel that I deserved to enjoy any aspect of life.

After accepting his death, I was ready to look at parts of myself that were appealing. Since I was learning to experience the world rather than rushing through it, I could linger as the runner ran through the crowd. I could feel his legs run like the wind, the wind blow against the sweat falling from his face. I could feel the drummer's hands loving the rhythm while touching the skin of the conga. I could begin to experience what it was like to love myself.

134

FAMILY DISCUSSION QUESTIONS
For Chapter Fifteen - *CELEBRATION OF JOY*

1. Rob dislikes zoos because they keep animals locked up. How do you feel about zoos?
2. Rob talks about being betrayed by his so called best friend. Talk about betrayal.
3. Rob learns that accepting loss is part of life. Have you had losses in your life? Do you think you have accepted them? How hard has it been for you to accept loss?
4. Rob feels free because he has reached a point where he is not dependent on anyone for direction or approval. Have you ever felt this way?
5. Rob discovers his own identity during this chapter. How did you feel about this?
6. Rob realizes that he has interests in common with his parents that increase his sense of connection with them. Have you had similar experiences?

CHAPTER SIXTEEN

WHERE EVIL LIVES

WHERE EVIL LIVES

CHAPTER SIXTEEN

WHERE EVIL LIVES

Rob is so exhausted that he decides to go to bed before The Ed Sullivan Show is over. He quickly falls into a deep sleep and has a dream with his father in a supporting role. In the dream, Rob is about nine years old, and he is playing right field in midget league. Midget league, is not to be confused with little league, because in midget league a kid can sit on the bench the whole summer-never get an at bat or play in the field for one inning. Little League is often more tolerant of kids who are not great or even marginal athletes.

Rob has been banished to right field, where the coach puts the worst player. He had started off the season hitting and catching well. Then for some reason, he would feel paralyzed each time he batted.

The games are played in summer heat and humidity at 6:30 PM. As soon as he gets up in the morning, Rob starts worrying about what will happen to him during that night's contest. His stomach used to cramp, and diarrhea would follow. Eventually, his mother introduced him to anti-diarrhea medication, medicine designed to keep his bowels from overflowing.

Rob runs slowly out to right field to begin the game. Fly balls, ground balls, line drives are all hit in his direction. He can see the ball and know he is supposed to move towards it, but his legs will not listen to his brain. His stomach is in knots as the inning finally ends. The coach just stares at him and the other players give him the silent treatment as he runs off the field and returns to the bench. His father and mother have shocked expressions on their faces while sitting in the stands. His father hated the competitiveness of midget league. His mother just felt sorry for poor Rob.

Rob is jolted awake by the intensity of the dream. It is morning. His pajamas are covered with sweat, and he feels that familiar anxious, gnawing feeling in his gut. Fears, worry, guilt, panic are all feelings that seem to be stirred up in his stomach.

He sits up in bed and swears that he can see all the trouble that is going on inside the lining of his intestines. The Silver Witch walks up to him and says, "All your troubles are your own damn fault, don't let anyone tell you different."

Supreme Guilt, the Wicked Witch stands beside the Silver one, and she is filled with misery. She is bitter about the raw deal life has dealt her. She informs Rob that he is to blame for all that is wrong and unjust in the world. The Blue Faced Ghoul joins this evil crowd and says, "You are to blame for your father's death. You could have done more to save him. You could have done less to aggravate him. You could have done more for your mother and sister. You never measure up. I hate to be the one that tells you, but no matter how hard you work, you cannot change the fact that you are guilty of all the crimes you are accused of today."

Hatchet Man tells Rob that he has never lived the correct way, that he is too stupid to know what is right. He says in a condescending voice, "You have disappointed all your friends, family, teachers, coaches, all those from whom you want admiration."

A greasy, disgusting slimy Black Bat lands between the two witches. The Bat is a disease ridden being that spreads his infection throughout the world. The Bat tells Rob that, "You can try as hard as you want, but you will never, ever measure up, not even close."

Soon other demons join the cast of evil characters. The Gremlin and The Two-Headed Monster come into the fray. Rob sees their mouths move in anger, but is too distraught to actually hear their words.

Rob reaches down and touches his abdomen while he watches the evil in front of him. He realizes that these demons and their evil are easily activated inside the middle of his body. He is surprised at how easy it is to come to this dreadful, horrible place and is painfully aware that it lives in his intestines.

He runs out of the house past the high school, past Main Street until he finds himself at the gates of the cemetery. The coffin is different now. It used to be a dingy, metal gray box, but now it is bright green and somehow alive. A large Eagle lands in the center of the graveyard. He is strong, brave and sees a bright future and Rob sees a bright future for himself. Rob thinks that it is really strange how he can travel from the bastions of evil to the gates of goodness in no time flat. How did he get to be so moody?

139

Puck is here with no worries and no thoughts of time pressures or impending doom. Puck is thinking about playing his flute and lying down in the noon-day sun. A beautiful woman with a sparkling crystal in her left hand comes near the coffin. She is free from dread and does not carry any burdens. She uses her crystal to guide the lost ones, and Rob certainly falls in the lost category.

Rob takes in her essence as he sits at her feet. He breathes her presence into his churning digestive system. She places her hand on his shoulder, and he feels the power of good, love and redemption wash over the evil that lives in his stomach. The pain in his gut vanishes while he watches the Crystal Woman's wings flap as she begins to ascend. Puck, the Eagle and The Crystal Woman are winged creatures and they honor their freedom by flying.

The Eagle says, "We are here today to celebrate the life and death of Rob's father." Suddenly Puck, The Crystal Woman and the Eagle lift Rob into the sky and fly him around the central New Jersey sky.

Rob can see the demons that are now outside the cemetery walls. He says, "It does not matter if I can see or feel the demons. They are always present; they are always inside and outside me. I can never escape them and I cannot run away from them. The more that I attempt to fight them or withdraw from their wrath, the worse my stomach feels. It ties into a series of little knots and spasms and cramps unpredictably."

From his view above the earth, he sees that a family of three has brought food to a celebration at the cemetery. They set up a picnic site and lay down an orange blanket to sit on. The baby sits between his mom and dad on this glorious day. Rob, while flying in the air finds himself inside the body of the baby. God, how his parents dote over him! Their eyes lovingly lock on to the baby's every nuance. Rob basks in the glow of his parent's warm emotional embrace. He is now the baby and also the teenager flying through the sky.

Then Rob finds himself inside the bodies of his mother and father coming together with the baby. Rob does not lose himself in this interaction. Instead, he becomes stronger and is able to connect with every living being in sight. He steps inside their shoes while still remaining independent from them. Then he takes a deep breath and announces to the world, "I can feel, hear, sense, even breathe in the truth that my parents really love me. I had to break through so many walls to discover this. I know now that I was unable to see the truth because of all the hurt that blocked my heart."

The celebration continues with Mexican Guitar Players singing praise to Rob's father's life and death. More winged creatures fly nearby the casket and honor the man whose life was cut so short. Neptune stands near the family of three. "Rob," he says, "you know that your father was able to experience this kind of joy in his life. I bet you did not know that joy could be expanded like a stone causing ripples in a pond. You did not believe true joy existed. You thought, at best, it would appear and just as quickly disappear. Your father knew the true essence of joy. He died before he could teach you this fundamental fact of life."

The Green Buddha silently joins the celebration while his peaceful energy goes out to the demons and the good ones. He is not driven like the jagged feeling that sometimes crops up in Rob's stomach. He is experiencing life as it is in the present moment. He does not judge others or worry. He tells Rob, "Fear, guilt, panic and evil live in your stomach and create havoc. Goodness, grace, and peace of mind live in your heart. During today's journey you traveled to both of them. What have you learned?"

COMMENTARY
CHAPTER SIXTEEN - *WHERE EVIL LIVES*

MAJOR CHARACTERS
Demons played by themselves
The Eagle played by himself
Puck played by himself
Crystal Woman played by herself
Family of Three played by Baby's First Steps
Mexican Guitarists played by themselves
Neptune played by himself
Green Buddha played by himself

This was the first time I brought up my stomach problems. It was also the first time I connected the presence of evil with any part of my body. I was able to explore the evil on a deeper level because of the work I had been doing facing the goodness. The goodness gave me a place of nurturing I could return to if the evil overwhelmed me. I was able to connect stomach distress with the evil figures. I learned that guilt; self-hatred and fear (denial of goodness) live in my stomach. I was able to move away from the evil by creating a totally different world. I did not attempt to escape the evil by withdrawal, burying or taking the figures out of the tray. I was able to experience the unfolding of happiness and joy.

This experience was different than merely getting a glimpse of happiness and then quickly moving on, focused only on the need to guard my environment. The joy began with Baby's First Steps and it continued to unfold and expand like ripples in a pond when a stone is thrown in. I identified this good world as my heart. When my heart opens up, fear slips away, self-hatred leaves the room and guilt disappears. I can look at the evil, but do not have to walk into its clutches. The evil and goodness live inside simultaneously. I also had a first experience with learning to live in the present rather than dwell on the past or worry about the future.

FAMILY DISCUSSION QUESTIONS
For Chapter Sixteen - *WHERE EVIL LIVES*

1.   Rob has wretched dealings playing baseball in "midget league". What have your experiences in organized sports been like?
2.   Rob talks about his quick shifting moods in this chapter. Does your mood ever suddenly change? How does that happen for you? How do your mood changes affect others that you are close to?
3.   How does your family celebrate major events?
4.   Rob realizes that his father did have joy in his life. Talk about joy. When do you experience joy?
5.   The Green Buddha does not judge others. Talk about judging others.

CHAPTER SEVENTEEN

WALKING WITH THE GODS

CHAPTER SEVENTEEN

WALKING WITH THE GODS

Rob wakes up after a marvelous sleep and watches the sun rise over The Atlantic Ocean. He has been in an almost continual celebration for some time now. He figures that working through all the doom, gloom, fear and self-hatred has called for all day, all night parties. The ocean is bright blue, and its giant waves rock the earth. He is relaxed and feels incredibly lazy today as he yawns to greet the morning.

A small woman wearing a black cloak and holding a huge diamond in her right hand wanders near the water. Rob wonders, but does not ask her how someone so diminutive can be strong enough to carry that big sparkling rock with just one hand. She lifts it high into the air, joyously offering it to all those who wish to join in the next wave of celebrating.

The large winged Eagle who is bold and fearless joins her. He comes and goes as he pleases. Rob takes a step into the Eagle's body and absorbs boldness and determination. Nothing will prevent the Eagle from living his dream. Nothing. The Eagle and the Jubilant Woman are related to each other. They are siblings and feel that all creatures of the universe are their brothers and sisters.

They are all staring at a snake eating himself and he is known as Infinity. He does not appear gross or disgusting. He is not in pain or agonizing over his plight. He says, "I am Infinity, the cycle of life that we all are a part of. The cycle of life will proceed no matter what. Guilt, fear or self-hatred cannot tamper with it. Rob, you cannot control the cycle of life any more than you can alter the time the seasons change every year." This comforts Rob, and he is relieved that he can let go of this burden.

The Drummer starts beating out a Puerto Rican rhythm on the conga. He focuses on his hand movements as slaps, palms and tones rain down upon the skin of the drum. He tries not to play too loud, just loud enough for his audience to immerse themselves in the music.

The Grim Reaper stands close to the shore. He is the death that moves from silence to screams as part of our daily existence. Rob is neither frightened nor enthralled by the Grim Reaper. He accepts him as being an essential part of life's landscape.

The Green Buddha and the Winged Lion join the party. The Buddha sits quietly and waits for words of wisdom that are sure to come. The Winged Lion is fierce enough to defeat all his enemies and can fly away when the battle is over. He is also waiting for words of wisdom.

The Fertility God rises up in the center of the party. He is dancing wildly as sweat pours down his face. Rob sees that the Fertility God is also courageous and is overjoyed with his own sexuality. He is half of the union that gives life. He is proud and amazed about the power he possesses. Rob is overcome with the joy of his own birth. He is so glad to be alive!

The words of wisdom will come from Rob today. He says, "All of you gathered today are both strong and tender. I feel that you have passed these qualities on to me, and I am forever grateful. I now know that I can have strength, joy, and happiness. I will also have to deal with fear, sadness, and death. I do not have to be half a person that lives only with demons riding his every thought. I used to believe that was my fate. Now there is so much of life to grab on to. I know now that it is possible to be fulfilled and that, in order for that to occur, I need to participate in so much. I need to drum, run, read, work on relationships, and fight against injustice. I want to find out who I want to be when I grow up. The healing continues and everything that has happened during this continual party points to a full and complete life. The Blue Ghoul, The Witch, The Raven, and The Grim Reaper are here. I am looking directly into all your eyes right now. I do not see the point of fighting you any longer. There is no need to bury or banish your demon energy. I will let you be. I will make peace with evil."

The Green Buddha is a being who is in and above the world. He transcends all hostility and conflict. He trusts that whatever tragedy occurs, a healing process will begin. The possibility that Rob will become a stronger, wiser and more complete person after his tragedy is one of the miracles the Buddha knows about.

Rob moves to the center of the beach where the sun is now at high noon, and he begins to speak, "I want to announce that I am forgiving myself for all the pain I have experienced up to this point. I realize some of the hurt has been internal and some outside of me. I am refusing to consume myself with

145

disillusionment and bitterness." He thinks about the Green Buddha's sense of wholeness and the Fertility God's joy and power. He has the sense that he can become more like them. He turns to the Green Buddha and says, "I want to walk with the Gods."

COMMENTARY
CHAPTER SEVENTEEN - *WALKING WITH THE GODS*

MAJOR CHARACTERS
The Jubilant Woman played by herself
The Eagle played by himself
Infinity played by himself
Drummer played by himself
Death played by the Grim Reaper
Green Buddha played by himself
Winged Lion played by himself
Fertility God played by himself

I had an ingrained belief system that the only "complete" people were television heroes. Although I knew some integral part was missing, I believed that I was complete in my demons-only world. I was complete in that terror-afflicted world. I did not think I had any other choices. I was stuck with the Witches, the Grim Reaper, the Blue Ghoul and their ilk for eternity. I believed that this was the complete world. I was now learning that demons were only a part of it. The goodness and joy of celebration is another part. I did not have to repress one to have the other. I could take in both.

The demons mixed in freely with the good figures. They did not have their own segregated space. The demons will always exist. What matters is how I interface with them. I have a choice as to whether I want them to rule the day or not. I also have the choice as to how much I want the goodness to get in. I was learning that I could expand and amplify my goodness experiences as long and deep as I wanted. I added one goodness figure after another. I was able to stay with and deepen the celebration of life. When the demons did enter, they were seen as nuisances, not instruments of destruction. I stayed with them a short time before I returned to the goodness figures.

I was also facing the fact that, in order to feel good, I had to get my needs met. This meant combining rewarding work with other pleasurable activities such as drumming, writing, and being with friends, in order to feel whole. When I felt whole I had the clear inner feeling that I could exist on a higher plane than I had before, a space of joy and spiritual awareness that the Green Buddha and the Fertility God represented.

FAMILY DISCUSSION QUESTIONS
For Chapter Seventeen - *WALKING WITH THE GODS*

1.   Rob meets the Eagle in this chapter. Nothing will prevent him from living his dream. Are you living your dream?
2.   Rob learns that the cycle of life will proceed no matter what. Do you agree?
3.   Rob loves to play congas (hand drums). Do you enjoy playing a musical instrument?
4.   Rob experiences the joy of being alive. Have you ever felt this way?
5.   Rob understands that he needs to take part in multiple activities in order to feel alive. Is this true for you?

CHAPTER EIGHTEEN

WHAT ABOUT THE WOMEN?

CHAPTER EIGHTEEN

WHAT ABOUT THE WOMEN?

It is getting cooler out as the sun fades away to a Jersey shore winter night. Rob can see stars in the sky, though they are dimmed by the overpowering lights of New York City. He slowly trudges across the beach. The wet and dry sand make his trek laborious. The moon, stars and city lights are so bright that he can see his reflection in the still part of the ocean. He sees his face look back at him. "Who am I?" he asks no one in particular. He is struggling to discover all the pieces of the puzzle that make up his being. Is he a tough guy? Is he a teenager of steel who never feels pain? Is he a coward, a weakling searching for cover? Is he strong enough to love all that he cherishes?

Up to this point in the journey, he has latched on to those who are masculine. Almost all of those he has met have been male; which include the demons and the good guys. Saint Martin, The Drummer, The Grim Reaper and The Two-Headed Monster have all been men.

What about the women? Although he has met female witches and a few other characters, he has not identified with them the way he has with the Runner, or even with the Blue Ghoul. Where have the women been, and why have they been reluctant to meet him? Or has he been afraid to meet them? He wonders, "Why have I been unable to connect with the feminine? Do I purposely keep them out of my life?"

He turns away from the water and starts to pace back and forth, oblivious to all the noise on the boardwalk. The world has taught Rob not to act, feel or be feminine. Acting like a girl was sure to bring ridicule and humiliation from all kinds of people. Embracing any facet of the feminine was definitely dangerous, because maleness equals strength and femaleness equals softness. This is a quality to be sought in girls, but never inside the male self. Masculinity must be observed at all times, and any behavior, thought, or words that were not strictly masculine were highly suspect.

Rob sits down on a sand dune and rubs his face while in deep thought. He realizes that he has lived by these rules, outdated rules that males are not

149

supposed to have any female characteristics. He is the only male in his family now, and he must uphold these masculine edicts or else. Or else what?

He hears splashing in the water and instinctively looks for the source of this sound. Without thinking, he strips down to his bathing suit and jumps into the salty water and swims out until he runs into a Mermaid and a Woman riding a Dolphin. The Mermaid looks pensive as she says to Rob, "It is alright to look at me. Please do not be anxious now. I am here to teach you that I am inside of you as well as outside.

She dives deeply into the water and Rob follows her down, but he can barely keep up with her because she is so swift. She is searching for pearls and he wonders what she will do once they are found. He swims as hard as he can, but to no avail, he cannot possibly maintain her pace.

He returns to the shore and lays down, exhausted and out of breath. He looks up to see a Silver Woman holding a staff in one hand and a crystal ball in the other. She asks, "Rob, do you remember what day it is? It is February 14, the anniversary of Lavya's death. Do you remember Lavya, Rob?"

Of course Rob remembers Lavya. She was the woman who first showed him what unconditional love was. She was like his second mother. The Silver Woman asks Rob to look further down the beach where a mother is awed by her son's walking for the very first time. Everyone on the beach and the busy boardwalk feels their love for each other. Rob felt that kind of love from Lavya, and he knew that no matter how much he messed up, no matter how much trouble he created, she would love him.

Suddenly he is in the hospital as Lavya lies on her deathbed. She is in so much pain because the cancer decided to spread across her body and into her brain. She is crying in anguish because she is devastated that her former husband did not come to visit her. Everyone else knew that he would never make that trip. Rob sees her wince with pain and feels her last anguished breaths. He wishes he could help her, but there is nothing he can do now. It is too late. He listens to her decades-old dreams being trampled by reality.

He cannot bear to watch her die. He runs out of the hospital until he reaches the familiar sights and smells of the Jersey shore. The salt air fills his nostrils, but there is no peace, as he asks the Silver Woman, "How could someone in so much pain be so loving?"

150

She leads him to a treasure chest filled with diamonds, pearls, and gold. She tells him that Lavya had a heart that contained all these elements and more. She says, "Lavya was unable to experience the richness of her own heart." Rob's eyes water up as the tears roll down his face. Lavya was cut off from the beat of her own pulse. It seems that she was only in Rob's life for a short moment. Rob remembers that when he was feeling hopeless, when all the doors seemed nailed shut, Lavya would turn on that big smile of hers and all the lights would go on. Suddenly life would be good.

An Angel with Wings flapping appears just as Rob walks under the boardwalk. The Angel is the best friend he ever had. She is a bright, strong ever-loving creature. She is Lavya's daughter, and while Lavya was dying, Rob ran away for months. Lavya's death made Rob think about his own father's death, and at the time he did not know what else to do but run far away. He looks at the Angel with shame in his heart. He had no idea how much he loved her and how close he came to destroying the best relationship he ever had. He really betrayed her by not being there during one of her darkest hours.

The Elephant Woman orders Rob into a courtroom. She informs him that he is charged with abandonment, and that he should feel ashamed of his actions. He admits that he is guilty as charged and begs for forgiveness.

The Green Buddha is the judge and he says, " The lesson here is that you know now that there is such a thing as true shame. When you hurt someone else, you deserve some of the suffering that comes from guilt." He says, "This is indeed true shame and you are deserving of it. This is unlike your previous ventures into shame where you blamed yourself for actions that were not your fault. This is different." Rob listens carefully and replies, "Yes, there are different kinds of shame. Some kinds of shame are lies and actually belong to others. This kind of shame is mine. This is the kind of shame that I own and need redemption from." He wonders how he might be redeemed?

The woman playfully riding a dolphin frolics in the ocean. She says, "Redemption is freedom from enslavement. You can be enslaved by others, and you can imprison yourself." Rob takes in the Dolphin Woman's teaching. She continues, "Your prison is the shame you carry. Its chains drape around your body like sausage casings. Your redemption will come from forgiveness and understanding. However, if you treat forgiveness and understanding as intellectual constructs, you will never by free. They are not mere words, but

151

openings to deeper worlds. You must swim deeper. You must return to the water to learn how to forgive and how to understand."

Rob drags his worn out body into the clear, salty ocean water. He swims through and over waves until he dives under. He sees a bright red, ancient Mayan mask. It is the face of a warrior. The Mayan warrior goes to battle. He fights for the right to survive, and never gives up.

Rob is drifting, alone and scared in the depths of the ocean. He is ashamed that he is not as strong and dedicated as the Mayan Warrior is. He is not fighting for what he believes in. He is not risking his life for any struggle. He feels useless and weak. A real man would join the Mayan warrior. A real man would be the Mayan Warrior. Since he is not prepared to risk it all, he feels guilt well up inside his stomach like a leaky hot air balloon. He continues to fall deeper into the water.

He longs for a rescue attempt. He feels frightened and alone. He sees The Loving Family of Three rush by in the currents. The unpredictable forces of the ocean cause mother and father to break away. Soon they are invisible. The baby stands terrified and alone. He has no one to protect him. He is being pushed around the water. It is like a tornado is battering his body.

Rob attempts to reach the baby, as they are both tossed around like airplane luggage. They end up inside a dark cave, and Rob feels his legs getting stuck in a crevice. The baby gets caught on some rocks. They see each other, but Rob cannot reach him. He yells out and asks the baby to be calm; help is on the way. He voices these words of assurance, though he has no reason to expect assistance.

Rob works his body back and forth in order to escape from the crevice, and his arms begin bleeding. He sees a monster, the Hatchet Man quickly swimming towards the baby. The monster is deranged and uncorked. He says, "I am the major force of the ocean's universe. It is my purpose to destroy all that appears innocent and weak." His large teeth reflect from the sun piercing through the water.

He sees the baby struggling in the rocks. The Hatchet Man's insanity comes to the forefront. He has the baby in his sights. He swims towards the rocks, raising his weapon of death as he goes. The baby cries out in panic. Rob shouts, "no, no!" At the last possible moment he frees himself from his prison

152

and manages to trip Hatchet as he goes by. Shiva, the Goddess with six arms begins pummeling Hatchet with all her fists until he is unconscious. Rob moves to the baby and frees him from the rocks. He picks the baby up and holds him with tired arms. The baby feels safe, cradled in his arms.

Shiva says, "That was a nice job, tripping Hatchet. You risked your life to save the baby. I know something about you. It is written all over your face. You love all the children. This is a special gift you possess. There are plenty out there who could use your sense of strength and kindness." Rob allows the water to wash over his body as the quiet of the sea engulfs him.

He begins talking to Shiva. He says, "Women are heroes too. You are smart as well as strong. I wonder how you know so much about me?" Although they are submerged underwater, she ignites a ring of flames around her. "This fire defines me. It is my guide and power. You have fought to deny that I am any part of you. Look at me! Look at my flames!" Rob stares at the ring of fire. Its blue, red and yellowness captivate him. Shiva is smiling. He feels like Shiva is standing inside him. Her smile is radiating his heart. The feminine is graceful, dynamic, sensitive, intelligent, and sweet. He feels the wall of denial falling by the wayside. The baby smiles with joy.

Rob and baby swim towards the light. Their heads pop through the water and the warm sunlight shines down on their faces. The baby gives Rob a hug and returns to his grateful parents who thank Rob profusely. He tells them the story of Shiva and how it was she who actually saved their son.

Rob feels that his journey is leading him into the present and future; that he no longer has to be held captive by the past. A majestic Eagle, a green Buddha, and Gods and Goddesses from all parts of the world surround Rob.

He looks at the world unfolding in front of him. The Fertility God is excited. Men, women and children are dancing and playing together. Gods and Goddesses are crying with happiness. There are five bridges connecting the entire world together. It is a great circle of life, the way it is most enjoyed. Rob walks out among the women, men, children, Gods, Goddesses and animals. He is a mere observer no longer. He shakes hands and hugs all those whom he approaches. Welcome to the world, Rob.

COMMENTARY
CHAPTER EIGHTEEN - *WHAT ABOUT THE WOMEN?*

MAJOR CHARACTERS
The Mermaid played by herself
Woman riding a Dolphin played by herself
Silver Woman played by herself
Lavya played by herself
Angel played by herself
Elephant Woman played by herself
Green Buddha played by himself
The Loving Family of Three played by Baby's First Steps

In this tray, Rob is no longer a teenager, and the experiences I lived in this tray and the following ones came from my early adult years. I was beginning to focus on the present and the future and was no longer stuck in the past. I walked out into the world and touched everyone. I stopped being an observer and became an active participant.

I learned about the feminine aspects of myself. Before this tray, I had the belief system that anything not masculine must be eradicated from my being. I learned that this eradication was neither possible nor desirable. The feminine, like the masculine can be bold and strong. I stopped denying the feminine side of myself in this series of sandtrays. Accepting the feminine was a crucial step towards integrating the different parts of myself, including the "evil" and the "good" parts.

Women have obviously played a great role in my life. One of those women was my mother-in-law, Lavya. (She actually died when I was in my mid thirties). The nature of the sandtray led me to connect different times of my life with certain experiences and that is why it she is included in this chapter. I was able to grieve her loss deeply. I got into the tragedy of her life and death. I learned more about the concept of unconditional love and what sense of self-confidence that brings.

I also re-experienced temporarily leaving my wife (the Angel) around the time Lavya died. I learned how afraid I was of facing loss. I learned the

154

difference between different types of shame. Some kinds of shame are lies; others are valid. I needed to let go of the false shame over my father's death, but to acknowledge and atone for abandoning Lavya and my wife. I was figuring out how to determine the real shame from the false.

FAMILY DISCUSSION QUESTIONS
For Chapter Eighteen - *WHAT ABOUT THE WOMEN?*

1. Rob realizes that up to this point in his journey, he has latched on to those who are masculine. He has not connected in the same manner with the feminine. Why do you think that is? Why is it a problem for Rob? How much has to do with the way Rob was socialized? Do you notice a pattern like this in your own life?

2. Have you ever felt that you were the "man" or the "woman" of the house? What has that experience been like?

3. Rob learns that the feminine exists inside him. Do you think that the masculine and the feminine exist inside all of us?

4. Rob talks about unconditional love in this chapter. What does unconditional love mean to you?

5. Rob states in this chapter, "Lavya was unable to experience the richness of her own heart". Do you know anyone like that?

6. Rob discusses the differences between true shame and the suffering that comes from guilt (where he blamed himself for actions that were not his fault). How do you feel about this? How can you know the difference between false and true shame and guilt?

CHAPTER NINETEEN

THE STILL WATER BEYOND SURVIVAL

CHAPTER NINETEEN

THE STILL WATER - BEYOND SURVIVAL

Rob walks in front of a large pit that is filled with water. He stands quietly by as terror fills the air. He feels drawn into the old ways of facing terror. It is so easy to return to the familiar, even though this worn out path overwhelms him. At this moment of the terror, he forgets beauty, he forgets the feminine, and he discards the goodness. His stomach starts to reel. He scans the horizon anticipating danger. He is powerless in preventing the demons from entering the world. They all come at once. The Hatchet Man, the Blue Ghoul, the Two Headed Lizard, the Three Headed Roach, the Screaming Gremlin, Bats, Rats and other vermin encircle him as they line up around the pit.

At this moment he believes they are plotting to chastise, condemn, humiliate, and guilt trip him. Rob experiences fear and shame immediately upon noticing their arrival. He believes they will call him names and put down all his efforts as meaningless and weak. He prepares to face them by tying himself to a stake while they hurl painful obscenities. He feels himself weaken as each insult travels deeper and deeper into his being. At this ritual's conclusion, he believes all the ugly words that flow from their gruesome mouths.

Sometimes, instead of just taking it, Rob fights back aggressively and with a mean spirit. He chooses to play their game of finger pointing threats. In the moment, retaliation seems so righteous, but a few moments after his "victory," hollowness set in. Nothing had been gained, learned or resolved.

Rob stares into the still water. He sees his reflection. He is pondering the drive behind this "You degrade me; I'll beat you" scenario. This is a saga of attacks and counterattacks. How many times has he repeated this bloodletting? He is aware that this activity has taken up much of his childhood and adolescence. The shame was its own reward. The vice grip of guilt was always at the end of the line of these battles.

He used to believe that experiencing deep humiliating shame was the path to truth. He used to believe that only by discovering the most intense self-disgust would he find resolution. The main focus of his life was to face how despicable a person he was. He found solace in losing his dignity. This was the only way he knew how to feel emotion, or what he believed emotion to be.

At the end of these battles, he would talk to himself. He would say, "See you really are a bad boy. You really are worthless. You will never measure up." These words would signal the end of the battle, and at that point Rob could wallow in self-pity. Self-pity became his identity.

Why is it so hard to move away from this? The water ripples as he questions the major premise of his being. Why am I so drawn to the anguish that shame, guilt, and humiliation bring? Is this the same sensation as being drawn to the still water? No, the water is beauty, calmness. The shame is masochistic and compulsive.

Rob takes a deep breath and steps back. He has to relive the shame over and over again. He thinks that the more he faces shame in this manner, the closer he will come to mastering the reason for its existence. If he masters the reason for shame's intrusion, then he will be free of it.

Rob sits down. He now knows that this attempt at mastery will never work in this manner. He glances up at the Hatchet Man, who says, "Yes that is one reason why you have followed this path, but your main purpose was to find words to hate yourself with. You confused sadness with self-pity, grieving with numbness, emotional release with self-destruction, truth with lies."

Rob looks at Hatchet differently. He is no longer afraid of him. Rob says, "Yes that was the old way of being. I guess I can always return to it. I have learned that I have choices."

Hatchet says, "We demons do not want to return to the old battles either. We want you to teach us what you have learned about this choices business."

Rob prepares to speak to all the demons. He looks into the deep, blue water. He is overcome with ripples of sadness, joy and love. "I cannot believe I am actually saying these words, but here is my proclamation. I have changed! The transformation took hold when the world of the feminine entered. No longer do I have to be hard, numb and closed off. The feminine is soft, sensitive and beautiful. We can now relate to each other differently. Demons, I want us all to hold hands and gaze into the still water."

158

The demons at first are reluctant to participate, but gradually join in. They look at their own reflections. Hatchet steps forward and says, "Rob, we can change too! We used to believe that if we did not hurt you, that you would face your father's death and that would be your ruination. We used to believe that looking too closely at your father's death would result in your demise. You have taught us those beliefs are false."

Suddenly death descends into the world. Death is one Large and one Small Grim Reaper, the Wicked Witch and the Witch with the Raven. Rob remembers how much he used to fear them. Hatchet says, "Let us all look at death." The Large Grim Reaper takes off his hood and reveals the smiling, wise face of an elderly man. "We are not here to terrorize you. We are part of life's cycle. We are born. We live through hard times. We discover joy and eventually we all die."

Rob places flowers of yellow and purple, bright colored fall trees and a box of sparkling jewels around Death and the Hatchet Man. He prays, "These flowers, trees and jewels are to celebrate the inclusion of all of you in my life. I will attempt to force you out no longer." He walks up to Hatchet and hugs him as his club; the weapon that has inflicted so much injury is dropped into the now warm water. We are honoring the end of the old way of being and the beginning of the new."

Rob faces the demons and death. He looks into all of their eyes. This is his method of reading the mystery that is unfolding before his eyes. He gathers up his strength and new- found confidence. He notices that they are surrounding the still water. They are mesmerized by its tranquility. He announces, "It is time to leave you now. I must step out of this world while you look at your reflections in the deep blue water. You have asked me to teach you how to live differently. The water will teach you."

Rob steps out of the world. The demons are no longer holding each other's hands. Facing the still water is an individual matter. Hatchet Man gazes into the pool. He is no longer stirring up turmoil. He is relaxed as he begins to talk. The others intently listen. "I am from a long line of beasts. My great grandfather, Hatchet Overlord, ruled our village with an iron fist. He created and enforced laws that were designed to prevent dissent or even a divergent opinion. I was taught to believe that to be different is to be a freak of nature. To be different leads to immediate punishment, banishment and painful death.

159

I always believed that it was my destiny to enforce great- grandfather's laws. As I stare into this beautiful body of water, I now question all of these long-held beliefs. I see myself sharp toothed, heavily armored, with this intimidating hatchet at my side. Why did I believe that to cry was weak, to have feelings was a sin, to admit you care, blasphemous? This armor feels like excess junk around my body."

He takes the armor off for the first time. He strives to remove it quickly, but is unable to because of its cumbersome bulk. It is finally tossed to the ground. His shoulders, neck, the back of his head are so relieved at the lifting of this burden. He continues, "I was not a person, I was a thing. The Hatchet-Overlord used me. I was a damn robot."

The Blue Ghoul is the next demon to speak. "I am lost. I do not have a clue who my ancestors are, or if I have any family at all. It has been my job to terrify. I have been so afraid of facing death myself. You all may think that is funny because it is pretty clear I look more like death than any of you. Yes, even you, Grim Reapers. It had been my job to remind others that death is a cruel, unnatural act that you must never face. I believed that if you faced someone else's death, you would die soon after. Where did I learn that garbage? What are the origins of this twisted belief? I have known men and women who have had a close family member die and never gotten over it. They remained despondent every day for the rest of their lives. They lived in such agony.

It is so tragic that anyone has to die. I don't want anyone to die. I don't want anyone to leave me. I am so frightened of being left alone. That is why my cat is always with me. I love my cat, but no one is allowed to know it, not even her. I am so tired of living this way."

He is perspiring, so he places his hand in the water and begins to wash his face. The blue color is coming off his forehead, his cheeks and his chin. He is struck by the image that reflects back from the water. He is no longer a blue ghoul. He is now human. He picks up his cat and holds her to his heart, and they both purr contentedly.

The Two-Headed Lizard then takes its turn at the base of the calm water. The two heads alternate barking out conflicting orders, statements and philosophies. The body of the lizard is exhausted by this babble. Finally one of the talking heads says, "Aren't you tired of fighting with me? I know I'm sick of these never-ending battles. I know it has been our purpose to confuse others.

160

We travel into their heads and argue with each other. Pretty soon they do not know what to believe. The result is that they become mistrustful of everyone. This has been our job." The second lizard responds, "That has been our job all right, and what a thankless endeavor it has become. Do you ever wonder why we do this? What is the purpose of creating mistrust?" The heads are silent for once as they ponder this question. They begin speaking with one voice, " If Rob begins to trust others, he may become close to them. What will happen to Rob if his friend dies! He will go nuts like he did when his Dad died. It is our job to protect him from that pain."

Hatchet, the Blue Ghoul, and the Two-headed Lizard raise their heads and look at each other. In unison they say, "We were protectors. We believed that we were keeping Rob safe from the horrors of death. Now we are learning that our tactics have been based on fear, when they could be based on the love we all feel for him. We believed that we were motivated by evil hatred. God, it's been such a horrible misunderstanding. We didn't know any better."

"Ha! I knew better than that," says the Bat. He focuses his red beady eyes on the water. "My sole purpose is to fire vile, disgusting, images into the mind of Rob. It has been my desire to make him believe that these images are accurate representations of him."

He pauses for a moment. The Bat, like the other demons has carried out his job without self-reflection. Staring into the still water now alters this pattern. "Yes, when I do my thing, Rob reaches the saturation level of self-hatred. It's funny. I know that all this disgust and vileness are false. It actually keeps Rob imprisoned, damned and under control. I have believed that he needs to be coerced by humiliation not to look at death or pain. I have attempted to make him believe that the more he focuses on his father's death, the more revolting his inner world would become. I had him convinced that this process would disintegrate his psyche. It was really my job to wash his brain and devour his soul.

I realize now that I did not care if he was happy. I did not care about his contentment or sense of security. All I wanted to do was to keep him alive. I was the siren that went off in his head. All I cared about was his survival. It was not in my capacity to see further than that. I want to discover what is beyond survival."

Somewhere off in the distance, Rob is bearing witness to this scene. Emotion comes up from his stomach and gets caught in his throat. He cries. "The demons and death have been trying to be my guards. I used to believe they were outside forces of evil. Then I came to believe that they resided inside me, and because of that I was damned. Now I realize that they were doing their best to protect me. They love me."

Night has fallen on the still water. Rob walks up to the demons. His arms have miraculously grown long enough to embrace all of them. He hugs them tightly and they hug back. "I love you too, I love you too." The crisp night air and the bright stars hold this moment for more than a heart beat.

COMMENTARY
CHAPTER NINETEEN – *THE STILL WATER* – *BEYOND SURVIVAL*

MAJOR CHARACTERS
Hatchet Man played by himself
Blue Ghoul played by himself
Two Headed Lizard played by himself
Screaming Gremlin played by himself
Death played by the Grim Reaper
Bat played by himself

In the midst of writing this entry, I experienced the unbelievably intense need to punish myself for the crime of being bad, not measuring up, not doing the right thing, and not doing enough. I was feeling an adrenaline rush while I said to myself, "I'm bad, I'm useless, I'm worse than worthless." However, none of these descriptions seemed to adequately define my wretchedness. I tried to go deeper inside in order to find those magic words. I felt that I deserved this self-torture and would begin to feel released from its grip when the tears started.

I used to believe that these were tears of sadness and grief, but they were actually tears of frustration and self-pity. The tears were my way of convincing myself and affirming that I really was an inherently loathsome person. I believed that self-torture was justified, because I was guilty of all the crimes and misdemeanors the demons accused me of. When the tears came, I would feel a short-lived sense of freedom, but this was not real freedom. It was merely a release of long pent-up frustration.

I did not know how to live any differently. I was so mixed up and had such a distorted sense of what feelings were and how they manifested. I learned there was a new way of facing the terror, that there was a new way of facing death. I could hold the demons in my heart instead of retaliating or withdrawing. I was extremely reluctant to go this new way. Part of me still believes that I do not deserve the peace and tranquility that the new way brings.

The new way begins by facing the demons with compassion instead of rage; reaching out rather than withdrawing, understanding instead of condemning. The old way promotes internal splits between the demons and Rob. They are either at war or unaware of each other's existence. When they are kind to each other, the split dissolves and a rich communing together is achieved.

At the end of the entry, the demons gazed at their reflections in the water. Each demon recited their job description, discussed their purposes in Rob's life and reflected on how they originated. The demons were actually protectors, not killers. They acted out of love, not hate. It appears all the demons could have stated the bat's words, "All I cared about was his survival."

The emotional impact and experience that the demons really loved me was a beautiful revelation. There was now the awareness that there was a life inside me that I could love, and that love could be reciprocated. It was equivalent to wrapping my own arms around my body. For that moment, I felt joy, warmth and security.

FAMILY DISCUSSION QUESTIONS
For Chapter Nineteen - *THE STILL WATER — BEYOND SURVIVAL*

1. Rob finds he can easily fall back into the old way of dealing with life. Do you ever find yourself falling back into old ways of acting that you thought you had changed?

2. Rob realizes that when he feels threatened, he verbally attacks others. Does this happen with you?

3. Rob talks about self-hatred in this chapter. Have you ever felt this way?

4. Rob realizes that he has changed in this chapter. Talk about times when you felt you had changed in a significant way.

5. Rob celebrates the inclusion of the demons into his life. How do you feel about this?

CHAPTER TWENTY

RING OF FIRE

CHAPTER TWENTY

RING OF FIRE

It is dark out. The only sound Rob hears is the trickling of water underneath the stone-cobbled bridge he is standing on. He sees two ancient buffaloes running towards a mountain. The buffaloes are a vanishing species in the world. Rob is pleased that they are joining him today. They are peaceful creatures who just want to be left alone to survive.

Out of nowhere a new demon appears. He comes from a place where violence is treasured. He knows only hate and vengeance. Rob looks at this demon in sheer panic. His eyes are the color of mustard gone bad. His teeth contain a wicked viciousness that is akin to a wild dog. He is known as Rabies. His skin is a bright, sickening yellow. He breathes heavily as he climbs on top of the mountain. He raises his nail-studded club above his head. He growls to let every one know that Rabies is in town.

Rob stands quietly on the bridge. He hears the water singing and glances downward. Death is flowing through the stream. It is not visible to the eye, but felt deeply inside. This death is sad, overwhelming all that has come before. Rob surrenders to his grief. The tears fall from his eyes. He does not wipe them away; he wants to hold this moment for all time.

A mother seal and her baby are swimming below him. A mother, father and child face each other and become one. Rob's feels the sadness erupt in his heart. He says quietly, almost in prayer, " I have not had a father for so long. What would it have been like to have a man to seek direction and love from? I am so worn out from relying on my own limited resources. What would it have been like to trust a man? What would it have been like to truly believe he had my best interest at heart? It has been so hard going it alone."

Rob says to himself, "Yes, I can forgive myself for having to live that lonely, frightening life as a teenager. I did not know any better. I did not know I had this rich world inside me that continues to get brighter." He commemorates letting go of this wound by picking up two handfuls of sand and dropping them in the stream. He watches the sand slowly float downstream until it can no longer be seen.

Peacock feathers and blue flowers are spread throughout the world. They honor all the pain, suffering and loss he has experienced. Rob rubs the peacock feather against his face. He realizes that beauty, softness and kindness are healing the hurt inside.

The demons enter in single file. The Hatchet Man, Two Headed Monster and Elephant Man face Rob and begin to speak as one. "We are demons. Our original purpose was to teach you that being in a place like this, surrounded by death, is wrong. You were not allowed to look at death because we did not think you were capable of handling it. We believed that being too close to death would drive you insane or kill you. It is so difficult to admit when we make mistakes, but indeed that was the case. You are strong enough to handle loss. You are strong enough to face death and all the sadness it brings. You have taught us that facing death expands our knowledge and decreases our fears. We admire you so much. We just wanted to take the time today to say we are sorry."

Rob's blue eyes are tear-filled, but bright. He smiles on the demons and they return his joy. Rob walks off the bridge. His feet do not touch the ground. The skier takes his place. An angel is nearby, kneeling and praying.

She says, "A long time ago, a man died. His name was Joseph Livingstone. He was a good man. He worked hard to take care of his family. He knew for quite a while that he did not have much time left to spend with his beloved wife and children. He did not have the words for what was happening to him. He wanted them to have all the things in life that he didn't. He wanted to give them stability, guidance and love. Joe's death was a tragedy, and the events that followed made life for his surviving family that much worse.

Dancing with her ring of fire, Shiva lights several candles at the foot of the mountain. One pink rose is placed on the bridge next to the skier. The Silver Woman, the Sand Painted Woman and Shiva stand in front of the candles. Shiva speaks. "Joe, when you died, I did not know what to do. I was so alone and left to raise two bewildered teenagers. No one seemed to understand what I was going through. There was no one there to comfort me. I could not really be there for the kids. I had trouble enough taking care of my own self and Joe, the pain I felt was excruciating. I tried not to let it show, but it was written all over the continuous frown on my face. I was devastated. I had nothing to look forward to, but I had to keep going in order to support the remainder of our family. I remember seeing you in the intensive care unit. I was not sure if you were suffering or not, but I told the children you were at peace. You had the accident and stroke, you were in the hospital two days and then you died. I never had the chance to tell you how much I loved you and how much I have missed you."

Shiva and Rob look at the Skier and Rabies. The Skier is the kind, gentle athlete part of Joe. Rabies is the fierce, rageful man who was out of control towards the end of his life. Rob walks up to Shiva and puts his arms around his mother. He says, "When I was fifteen, I had no idea how hard it was for you. I was so numb; I did not know how it was for anyone. Mom, I want to thank you for taking care of my sister and me by yourself. I had no idea how difficult a job that was in the best of circumstances.

You managed to go to work everyday and make sure that our basic needs were met. I know now that you had no support in the community. It would have been easy to give up, but you were strong enough to overcome that void."

There is darkness everywhere except where Rob and his mother are guarded by the ring of fire.

COMMENTARY
CHAPTER TWENTY - *RING OF FIRE*

MAJOR CHARACTERS
Two Ancient Buffaloes played by themselves
Rabies played by himself
Loving Family of Three played by Baby's First Steps
The Demons-Hatchet Man, Two Headed Monster, Elephant Man played by
themselves
Rob's Mother played by Shiva

I realize that I have an ongoing need to return to the funeral scene and recreate it to my specifications. This not only heals the wounds, but also opens my psyche to fresh knowledge.

This was the first time I could stand in my mother's shoes. This process allowed me to empathize with her plight , as I never did before. As a teenager, I took so much for granted. I had no idea what it took to go to work and attempt to function while in the midst of intense grief. Now I can thank her for her persistence and strength. I experienced what it was like for her to lose a husband. The loss of a father was devastating, but the loss of a husband may have been worse. This is a new awareness for me.

FAMILY DISCUSSION QUESTIONS
For Chapter Twenty - *RING OF FIRE*

1.   Rob talks about endangered species in the world. How do you feel about this issue?
2.   Rob experiencing letting go of the wound he had carried for so long. Are there wounds that you are carrying around with you? How do you feel about letting go of them?
3.   The demons apologize to Rob during this chapter. How do you feel about this?
4.   Rob's mother talks about her feelings here, the first time we have heard from her. How does hearing her side change your view of Rob's story?
5.   Rob empathizes with his mother in this chapter. How do you feel about this process?

CHAPTER TWENTY- ONE

THE NEXT BEST BIG RUSH

CHAPTER TWENTY-ONE

THE NEXT BIG RUSH

Rob is standing in a vast desert. He is bored. Boredom happens between the elation of the joy and the trauma of the evil. Boredom is a restless, gnawing nothingness. Rob is pacing up and down. He wants to do something, but what? This tedium has an agitated edge. He sees Rabies enter the center of the desert. He is immediately buried with layers of dry sand. Rabies is comprised of many elements. He is fierce, powerful, dangerous, evil and strong. Today, he is death covered over, a death that can be seen, but not felt. There are other coffins and caskets nearby.

An Eagle flies past Rob. He is also restless as he stares at a mirror in front of him. He examines his wings, feathers and beak. He longs to fly somewhere for something, but remains clueless as to what or when. The Elephant God stomps around the desert looking for some action. He is seeking a distraction from this dead, anxious feeling.

Rob walks around the desert searching for a sign as to what to do now. He is not satisfied, unfulfilled and looking for the next big rush. He picks up an orange pill and ingests it without water. His vision, hearing and sense of balance slowly become distorted. He starts to worry about what is happening to his mind. The fear inside reaches a fever pitch. He feels unprotected and does not know how to stop the rumbling in his stomach and the aching of his head. At the same time, he is striving for enlightenment. He hears the voices of Bob Dylan and Jimi Hendrix float from the stereo speakers. Surely, they know the answers. They know how to find peace. Rob listens between the lyrics to the soaring guitars and pounding drums. Each note creates a different colored shade in his head.

A rainbow with a background of pale yellow light captivates him. Bam! Panic hits him. He is not allowed to be so unguarded. He must open his eyes and prepare for danger. This is his destiny. He opens his eyes and sees horrible insects and spiders crawling around the space in front of him. He wants to run but cannot move his legs. He is so frightened, and the more fearful he is, the more bugs rush around him. He wonders, "Why are these bugs here?" There is no one to answer his anguished questions. He is alone and terrified. He notices that his hands are cold as ice. He manages to get up and walk away. The bugs do not go with him.

He feels himself begin to rise out of his body. He is scared but is powerless to do anything about these phenomena. He travels up past moist clouds, into a blue sky that turns to a night filled with stars. He continues traveling upward until pink clouds that look like cotton candy surround him. He feels so tranquil as heat overcomes him in the form of a whiteness that he has never seen before. This white is pale and bright simultaneously. The whiteness is reverberating like an earthquake and washing over him like a flood.

At the peak of the whiteness, Rob finds himself falling past the pink clouds, past the night sky, past the blue sky and white clouds until he lands smack in the middle of the desert.

He is standing between two Grim Reapers. Death has always followed him. He wonders if he just died, went to heaven and came back to earth. The Grim Reapers are stoic, stiff and heartless. They raise their right arms and point. They say, "Death is to be feared, death is to be buried and covered up. You must learn to escape death's messengers. You must never face death. You must repress and deny any thoughts, ideas or feelings about it."

Rob is so tired and confused. He is raw. His nerve endings need soothing, but he feels alone and isolated. The worry feels like shards of glass stuck below the surface of his skin. He is crying tears of desolation. It is time to give up. Rob has lost the last battle of the war. He is a young man in his late teens. He looks at himself in the mirror. His hair is scraggly and he has huge boils on his face. He has lost a lot of weight from a body that could not afford to lose much. He was past self-pity. He sees himself laying on a curb with a cheap bottle of wine in one hand and a greasy, chicken fried steak in the other. He believes that this is his true destiny, to be a loser.

The peaceful Buddha sits down in front of him. Rob finds the energy to look up at him. The Buddha has lived for millions of years. Rob connects with his serenity. Rob doubts that he could ever be so at rest. The Buddha speaks, " When you left home for the first time there was no security, no direction, no faith. You were living in troubled times. You were paying the price of not dealing with your father's death. You tried to distract yourself by failing in college and taking a multitude of drugs. The more you attempted to push death

172

down, the more fearful and defenseless you became. The Grim Reapers became more rigid as you grew from a late adolescent to a young man."

An Angel with Praying Hands sits near Rob. She says, " Let us pray now. It has been so horrible to be filled with this terror day after day. No one could really help you. You did not know what was wrong. You did not have the words to ask for help. All you could do was to follow the terror until it robbed you of your strength and humanity. Let us now recognize the toll this prolonged agony has taken on your mind, body and spirit."

Rob walks up to the burial ground. He bends down and begins digging with his hands. He now sees Rabies' head. He is alive. The sand did not kill him. Rob now knows that you cannot kill death. Pretty soon Rabies is completely uncovered. He says, "I am part of your world just as life is. Your fear of me creates a monster, but I am not really a salivating creep. I am just like you. I am a part of the cycle that comes into the world and then eventually leaves. This is just the way it is."

Rabies is now on top of the mountains with red stones surrounding him. He continues, "Life is right in front of you. Look!" A mother, father and infant son play with each other. "Time stands still for them. They are living in the present. They are not worried about what they will miss when their gathering ends. They are appreciating every moment now."

Rob looks at Rabies, who says, "When the energy of forcing down death is voluntarily released, something new happens." Rabies is no longer dreary death. He is now a wise one. He says, "Who knows what happens when you die?" Rob wonders what happened to his father.

Rabies quietly delivers the most important speech of his life, "Son, I left you so suddenly. I know you have been without me for so long. I do not want you to worry about me now. When you worry about my soul, I become stuck between two worlds. One world is peaceful and allows my spirit to fly. The other world is a place between death and this spirit-flying place. I want to tell you that I have found peace. This in-between world is not bad, but I would rather be at rest. You can help me do that by letting me go." Rob takes a huge breath, exhales and raises his arms to the sky. He sees his father's spirit rise up to the sky and beyond.

COMMENTARY
CHAPTER TWENTY ONE - *THE NEXT BIG RUSH*

MAJOR CHARACTERS
Rabies played by himself
Death played by two Grim Reapers
Peaceful Buddha played by himself
Angel played by herself

Boredom was the first topic of the day. Boredom had played a huge role in my life. For starters, I could not distinguish between being relaxed and bored. How much of my boredom was teenage angst and how much was the boredom a defense against dealing with the painful feelings concerning the loss of my father? I learned today that the restlessness was more a defense.

The boredom led me to increased drug use. One of those experiences is shared in this entry. I don't think I ever had a good acid trip. I could never be calm. I was always guarding myself against unforeseen danger. This guarding led to intense fear that created very scary visual hallucinations.

I had the experience of leaving my body and going to heaven. Is this what will happen when I really die? No one knows. Drugs intensified my sense of isolation and loneliness. Unlike many of my peers who were taking LSD for fun, I dropped the tabs to find myself. I thought acid was the path to truth. Maybe it is, but I sure got waylaid in the detours. Drugs were also used as a method to repress any pain, from my father's death or any other cause.

My father's spirit talked to me directly. He told me that I had a role in letting him go. I began to realize that letting him go is a continuous process, not a one-shot deal like in a Hollywood movie.

FAMILY DISCUSSION QUESTIONS
For Chapter Twenty-One - *The Next Big Rush*

1.   Rob has a drug experience during this chapter. Talk about what you know about drugs.
2.   Rob feels unprotected and extremely vulnerable. Have you ever felt this way?

3.   He listens to music in his search for enlightenment. Do you ever listen to music for that purpose?

4.   Rob experiences terror during this chapter. Have you ever felt this way?

5.   Rabies transforms in this chapter. How do you feel about this?

6.   Rob's father talks about being stuck between two worlds. Have you ever felt that way?

CHAPTER TWENTY-TWO

EXPLODING ENERGY

CHAPTER TWENTY-TWO

EXPLODING ENERGY

Rob watches Rabies march up a mountain in the middle of the desert. Rabies is frothing at the mouth. He radiates unpredictable craziness. He swings his club at invisible enemies. His groans sound like anguished cows. Spit is flying from his parched lips. This unharnessed energy creates fear in the valley below. A casket is revealed in the direct vision of Rabies. This sight causes him to become angrier and more dangerously out of control. He sees monkeys piled on top of each other. He wants to annihilate them. There is no rhyme or reason to his madness.

The Winged Lion flies in at the foot of the mountain. He yells up at Rabies. He says, " I know you are furious, I know you want to seek and destroy, but you have no direction. Will you let me help you?" Rabies stops all his meaningless gyrations and stares at the Lion. The Lion continues, "It is cold here. I am going to gather some wood in order to start a campfire." Night is falling rapidly. The heat from the sun is quickly fading.

The fire's warmth and colors have a mesmerizing effect on Rabies. Shiva, the serene Buddha and the Little Snail join the Winged Lion. Rabies, from the mountaintop says, "I have spent my life striking out at any object that gets in my way. It has not mattered what that object is. It has been my job to seek and destroy, like an unguided missile. I wonder, do I have any other purpose in my life?"

Shiva, with her own ring of fire responds. She says, "There are lots of battles that need fighting today."

Rabies roars, "Let me at them, who are they?"

Shiva says," But Rabies, what do you believe in? Why do you fight so much?

He replies, "I fight, I hit, I pummel to protect myself from being injured or killed. Anyone who stands in my way is asking for trouble in a big time way."

Rabies is sad now. "I want to be strong, I want to find somebody to protect. I am tired of all this random attacking."

The Buddha declares, "You can protect us! You can defend all of us that live in the valley." Hatchet Man, a Beautiful Woman, another Buddha, and the Drummer all join the others. The Buddha continues, " Rabies, your name does not fit you any longer. From now on you will be known as the Warrior King. You can protect us from the forces that hate."

The newly anointed Warrior King stares into the fire. He comes down the mountain and joins his new found comrades. He says, "There are those in the world who hate us because of the color of our skin or because our sexual orientation is different, or they hate us simply because we are women. I pledge to stand by all of you." He then marches up the mountain. He raises his club in triumph.

The Warrior King walks down to the casket. Demons and the good ones surround them. The Wicked Witch the Blue Ghoul, and the Three-Headed Monster join the Peacock, and two American Indian Dancers.

Rob sees a Green Buddha, an Elephant Goddess and a Pink Pyramid on the other side of the mountain. He goes to them. The Buddha says to Rob, "We are going to teach you what we know about death. You are now ready to take in this knowledge. Death, as you know is part of life. It is not a separate entity. Life is endless. It goes on forever. However, your life span is very short compared to infinity. It is important that you live every second and enjoy all that is inside and outside you. I know you worry about what will happen when you die, what happened to your father when he died. When your body dies, its spirit will either go to heaven or return to earth. Your spirit will live on as your father's does. You can feel his presence when the time is right for this miracle to occur. Is your father alive somewhere? Here on earth in some life form? Or is he totally eliminated from any level of existence?"

The Elephant Woman says, "You are not ready to know the answer to this. Someday you will. However, if he is no longer alive on any plane, he found peace when his heart stopped beating."

Rob walks through the desert. He sees a clearing and then thousands of lights. He is now in the city he loves, San Francisco. AIDS is striking down young men and women in the prime of their lives. His friend Kevin is one of the

178

disease's victims. A foggy morning has given way to a sunny June afternoon. The memorial service takes place in a church near Rob's community. Friends and family from all over the country are in attendance. The minister asks all those who would like to speak to do so. Several folks walk in front of the podium and talk about the life of Kevin. Rob wished that this could have happened at his father's funeral so many years ago. There was music playing that Kevin loved, and stories of his wild antics are being told. Kevin was one of the funniest persons ever to have lived. He was compassionate and always lively. It was truly a crime to have all that energy snuffed out by this cruel disease.

Rob goes to his father's grave. He places white, yellow and red flowers on it. A red hummingbird drinks the nectar from the flowers while his body hovers in the air. Rob looks at the bird's face and swears he sees a smile there. "Kevin," Rob says, "wherever you are, I hope you are forever laughing."

COMMENTARY
CHAPTER TWENTY-TWO - *EXPLODING ENERGY*

MAJOR CHARACTERS
Rabies played by himself
The Winged Lion played by himself
Serene Buddha played by himself
Shiva played by herself
Hatchet Man played by himself
Green Buddha played by himself
The Warrior King (formally Rabies) played by himself

Rabies was transformed into the Warrior King. He learned to have a direction for his angry energy. He decided that he would protect his flock against racism, sexism and homophobia.

Later, I went to my friend Kevin's memorial. I could not help but compare this event to my father's funeral. My father's funeral lacked celebration, understanding of his life or compassion for his survivors. Kevin's memorial had all of those elements and more.

FAMILY DISCUSSION QUESTIONS
For Chapter Twenty-Two - *EXPLODING ENERGY*

1. Rabies seems to be angry for no reason. Do you ever get angry and don't know why? What do you do when you feel like that?
2. Rabies realizes that he fights in order to protect himself from being hurt. Can you relate to this?
3. Rabies eventually finds a different purpose, to protect the others. How do you feel about this? Do you think Rabies can do a good job of this?
4. Rabies gets a new name - Warrior King. How did this happen?
5. What does Buddha teach Rob about death? What do you think of the Buddha's teaching?

CHAPTER TWENTY-THREE

VOICES OF TRUTH

CHAPTER TWENTY-THREE

VOICES OF TRUTH

Majestic and timeless icons surround Rob. He knows they are Gods and Goddesses. He has stepped into a New World where the air is clear, the weather balmy and the ocean blue. He senses that he has entered this world in order to learn. He has no idea what the nature of the lessons will be. What makes these beings Gods and Goddesses? Are they perfect entities unto themselves? Are they merciless fighters with no compassion for those less noble? Are they true heroes and heroines? Do they like common everyday people? It is time to find out.

Rob turns to look into the faces of the Forty Thousand-Year-Old Mesopotamian couple. They are joined together as one. Their sides have merged into each other. They are holding each other's hands while their arms are draped across their backs. They are in love. There is no force in nature that can destroy the love they share. They trust each other implicitly. Nothing in the universe can tear them apart.

The couple are neither laughing nor crying. They are not stoic or withdrawn. They observe every aspect of life. They do not get waylaid or distracted by crisis. They know they have each other, always. They have reached a point where suffering is unnecessary; where learning is an exuberant experience; where the past does not have to be continually analyzed; where fear is a forgotten construct.

They do not believe in war. They are wise and patient. They are the source that loves unconditionally. This source lives within all of us, but somehow gets battered away. Their force overcomes the anguish and fighting in the universe.

Rob discovers the Mayan Gods and Goddess. The Gods are dressed for battle and are in a fighting stance, but they are not vicious or vindictive. They only fight in self-defense, if their people or lands are about to be devoured by their enemies. They take no pleasure from war.

The Male Gods are protectors. They draw lines in the sand, not as dare-macho-boasting, but as an unmistakable statement of truth. "If you cross this line

182

without my permission, it is clear you mean to do my people harm. I will have no choice but to stop you."

The Mayan Goddess is as strong as the men. She has both her arms raised, holding up the entire world. Her eyes are closed. She knows that male protective energy is necessary, but she will not accept aggressive raping of the land and people. She is forgiving and compassionate. She is feminine and powerful. She never gives up her quest for world peace. Her arms are raised in prayer, honoring all the seen and unseen spirits of life.

The Garuda is a Polynesian god. His skin is colored in reds, yellows and oranges. He has a shocking appearance. His red markings look like fire, as if he were all ablaze. He is burning with intensity. He looks crazed and about to lose all semblance of control. He is frightening.

Rob looks up at his contorted face. Garuda says, "We all need to take a good look at the way we live our lives. Have we been charitable? Have we been too wrapped up in our own lives to give to others?" Garuda is not a guilt god. Guilt does not come from gods. It is humans' misinterpretation of Garuda's message. He is not asking us to beat ourselves with clinging hair shirts. He is not seeking punishment. He is merely asking us to look outside of ourselves. He is asking, "Will it be a better world if we help out those less fortunate then ourselves?"

Look at the monkeys all piled on top of each other forming a pyramid! There must be dozens of them. They are smiling with glee. They are all from different villages. They never met before today, yet they trust each other with their lives. The monkeys are holding each other up by stepping on their brothers and sisters shoulders. One misstep could cause the entire pyramid to come tumbling down. They trust each other's level of strength and intentions. They know they have to cooperate with each other in order to survive and achieve.

Krishna and his Consort from India stand before Rob. Krishna is playing a flute and they are dancing. Joy is written all over their faces. Their joy is not wild partying. They are on permanent vacation. They also trust each other implicitly. This god and goddess give the message of the importance of play and relaxation in our lives. Life is just not to be endured, but to be enjoyed through playing.

The Ivory Buddha is carrying his laughing daughter on his back. Rob notices that they are both laughing. This is a masculine connection with children. Out of this bond come patience, care-taking, feeding, washing, teaching, fun loving, and imparting wisdom to the little one. The Buddha appreciates his role in fatherhood. He loves his daughter. She is laughing and carefree. She feels safe, so safe that she does not need to know the meaning of the word protection.

The sight of the Snake Buddha initially startles Rob. She has a snake draped around her body. The snake is venomous, filled with poison in his fangs. The Buddha trusts the nature of the poisonous snake. She has tamed the wild snake through powers of healing rather than coercion. The snake was striking out because of fear and anger. The Buddha helped heal his rage.

Rob realizes that the Warrior King has been transformed into a god. The Warrior King looks around at the other Gods and Goddesses. He clears his throat and begins talking in a new, deeper voice. "I am the god of change. I was once a hateful, rageful beast. I have shown the world how much change can occur. I am now a kind, understanding leader who has within him elements of all the gods and goddesses that are with us today. We all have the realm of the Gods and Goddesses inside us."

The Drummer plays softly. His rhythm begins slowly. The sound is as soothing as it is powerful. Its richness fills the entire world with joy and reverberation. Words float between the beats. They say, "The Gods and Goddesses are love, and love can never die."

COMMENTARY
CHAPTER TWENTY THREE - *VOICES OF TRUTH*
MAJOR CHARACTERS
Mesopotamian Couple played by themselves
Mayan Gods and Goddesses played by themselves
The Garuda played by himself
Monkeys in a Pyramid played by themselves
Krishna and his Consort played by themselves
Ivory Buddha with Child played by himself
Snake Buddha played by herself
Warrior King played by himself
The Drummer played by himself

I learned more about the Gods and Goddesses. I learned that they live within all of us and represent universal truths. These truths never die, no matter how much destruction occurs in the world. These truths get misplaced and misinterpreted. The truth underlying all is, God is love.

The eternal wisdom of the Gods and Goddesses became a source of strength for me. Although I could not always hold on to their truths, they guided me at crucial times. Because of their teachings and the other lessons I had learned, each time I found myself back in the cycle of guilt and despair, I was able to recover more fully and move a little higher. This happens dramatically in the final chapter.

FAMILY DISCUSSION QUESTIONS
For Chapter Twenty-Three - *VOICES OF TRUTH*

1. Rob learns that there is no force in nature that can destroy the power of love. Do you agree?
2. The Mayan Gods and Goddesses practice self-defense. In fact, that is the only situation in which they will fight others. Do you agree with this philosophy?
3. Rob experiences the Mayan Goddesses as equal with the Mayan Gods. How do you feel about this?
4. What is the Garuda's message?
5. What do we learn about the pile of monkeys?

CHAPTER TWENTY-FOUR

I NEVER SAID GOOD-BYE

CHAPTER TWENTY-FOUR

I NEVER SAID GOODBYE

Rob walks past bright colored stones in the road. They are shiny turquoise and bright blood red. He stops when he almost falls in a giant hole. The ground is moist. The space in the ground is large enough for a body. It is a grave, his father's grave. A cheetah screeches behind him.

Rob looks at the empty grave. He remembers his father getting sick, going to the hospital and suddenly dying. Rob says, "I never had the chance to say goodbye. I was not allowed in the intensive care unit. I have no mental picture of what my father looked like when he died. Whenever I reach this point, I feel so stuck. I only recall some of our final days together."

It is a hot and muggy New Jersey summer day, and Rob is lying on the bed in his room. He hears footsteps running up the stairs. He hears labored breathing. His father abruptly opens the sliding door to his room. He is now standing in the middle of the linoleum floor. His father's hair is wild and uncombed, flying in every direction. He is wearing a worn flannel shirt and chino pants with holes in them. His glasses are on crooked. His eyes are on fire. He looks crazed.

Rob tenses up his body. He knows that his father is preparing to hit him, like so many times before. Rob has no idea what he did wrong. His father is past the point of using words to express his rage. He keeps moving towards Rob. There is violence in the hot air. His father pulls his hand back, ready to strike his son. He does not care what part of his body gets wounded. Rob must be punished. He is bad. He is a rotten kid. Here comes the hand ready to slap Rob down.

Rob does not plan for what happens next. Before he knows it, his right fist is reared back. He lets it fly right into his father's midsection. His father doubles up in pain. His wild, insane eyes suddenly change. They take on a look resembling defeat. His father grabs his stomach with both hands. He clearly has the wind knocked out of him. Rob expects retaliation. He tightens his entire body. His neck is stiff as a piece of thick steel. He waits for his father to charge, but instead of attacking, he backs out of the room the way he came in. He now has his head bowed and slowly walks down the stairs.

The retaliation never comes. His father never really looks at him again. Whenever Rob attempts to look into his father's eyes, he either turns away or stares blankly through him. Rob no longer exists. It is as if his father has disowned him. Shortly after, his father dies.

Rob is filled with guilt. "I hit my father. I am so bad and evil. He dealt out the ultimate punishment. He ignored me. He pushed me away because I was such a disappointment to him. I never measured up to what he wanted me to be. I hit him. He stopped interacting with me and then he died. I never knew why he stopped talking to me. I could not understand our strained relationship. I did not understand his life, and I could not fathom his death. Boom! Right in the middle of an upheaval called adolescence he left me for good."

The Vain Woman stares into a mirror as she walks up to Rob. She is so sarcastic. She taunts Rob; "You are such a weakling. So your father died. You use his death as an excuse not to get on with your life."

Rob believes the Vain Woman. He sees a black cloud descend on his shoulders. The black cloud has been with him the day he hit his Dad. It is a cloud of burden he carries every waking hour. He spends hours trying to find answers to his anguished pleas. "Why did he just walk away? It would have been better if he kicked my ass. Walking away left me hurt and confused. Why did he never connect with me again? This only makes the abruptness of his death harder to take."

Rob looks at the multi-colored stones in front of him. The red ones are the blood that stopped flowing in his father's arteries. The turquoise stones are the vast emptiness in the universe that came from his death. The Grim Reaper is the burden Rob bears of blaming himself for being a bad kid. He had the audacity to punch his father in the stomach. He had no respect for him. He should be punished for not respecting his father, but he never was punished for this sin.

The fall trees surrounding the grave feel claustrophobic. The trees tell him he is not allowed to leave this space. He is forced to face the Grim Reaper, the Cheetah, the bright colored stones and the grave itself. He continues to beat up on himself. He hates himself for hitting his father. He is angry his father did not reprimand him. He is confused as to why his father never talked to him again.

188

All he is left with are painful memories and assumptions and questions of why. He never finds solace in these questions, or any of the answers he needs so badly.

He looks at the grave and is filled with the familiar, disappointing numbness that comes from this process. He yells at the Cheetah and screams at the Grim Reaper. "You call me names, you shame me into submission. I hate you." Tears of frustration fill his eyes. He hopes the tears will bring relief. He hopes they will deliver answers that never come.

His father stands near the grave. He is wearing the same clothes as before, but even more disheveled. · He has had the same clothes on for twenty-five years. He has floated around the universe in an angry and confused state. Death has not been kind to him. He has found no peace in death.

Rob looks at his father. He is pitiful. He is ragged. He has a blank, catatonic cast to his face. His crooked glass lenses are now cracked. Rob says, "You are a pathetic and cruel excuse for a father. How come you never talked to me again after I hit you? Why did want to strike me in the first place? What in the world did I do that was so wrong? Why did you die and leave me all alone? Why did you hate me so much? Please, please tell me!"

His father turns from Rob and walks away. Rob follows closely behind him. He attempts to grab his arm. Air is all that he grasps. His father has vanished once again.

Rob sees the Fertility God and Goddess come into the horizon. They are making love. The God is strong, kind and dependable. The sight of the God causes Rob to long for all that he has missed. Rob has not felt secure. He did not have a father he could count on. He had this erratic man in his life who thoroughly confused him.

He thinks, "My father beat me, he despised the ground I walked on." He suddenly realizes that the most intense pain does not come from the beatings or the verbal abuse. It comes from the silence of his father's withdrawal. Rob realizes that he has been fearful of others' replicating his father's silent stare. He has struggled all his life to keep from being treated this way.

Rob looks at pictures of him and his father seemingly having fun together. Rob does not remember any of these so-called good times. The pictures do not resonate with him. He has no memories of the good times. He has no loving connection with his father.

What he does have is bitterness. He has been stuck in bitterness for years now. The black cloud of burden weighs him down. His back is so heavy he falls on the ground and lapses into a fitful sleep.

When he awakens, it is cold out. The land is vacant before him. He has never felt this lost before. All the trees, stones and creatures are gone. Once again he is all alone with only his fears to misguide him. There is no hope. There is no possibility for happiness. There is only despair.

A black man dressed in a sacred robe now stands before him. Rob asks, "Who may you be?" "I am St. Martin De Porres, patron saint of the lost souls." Rob says, "Well you have come to the right place. Can you help me overcome my bitterness?"

There is a long silence before St. Martin responds. He asks, "What is the purpose of the bitterness?"

"The purpose? There is no purpose. It just lives inside me every waking minute and I am sick of its controlling, putrid taste," replies Rob.

"Do you think getting angry is going to set you free?" asks St. Martin. "I do not know what freedom is", declares Rob.

St. Martin asks Rob to sit for a moment and focus on his sermon. "Try not to judge what I say. Be open to my words." Rob settles down into a comfortable position. St. Martin begins. "Open your eyes. See what is really here today." Rob looks around. He sees a galloping Bright Blue Horse. It is so beautiful and triumphant. A Mother Seal with her Baby relaxes by a pond. Bright colored trees surround him. They open up his spirits. They touch his heart.

A huge red rose lands right in back of his father's grave. This rose is his heart. St. Martin continues. "Where does bitterness live? Does it live in your heart? No, it does not, but it blocks all feeling from the heart. Bitterness is only exaggerated numbness. It can live in your head or your stomach. The bitter place is where you end up when you feel stuck. Hatred towards life overcomes you. Your mouth hangs in a scowl and the lines in your face become like leather. You lose the ability to love. All that is feminine is lost. The heart becomes a forgotten vessel."

Rob runs up to the giant red rose. Its smell is divine. He feels his heart opening up. He suddenly feels so alive. There is a man standing by the grave. He has a new corduroy sport coat. His shirt is freshly pressed. His hair is slicked back. He has a new pair of glasses. He looks relaxed. The man is his father.

Rob takes a deep breath. "Dad, I have some questions I need to ask. Please do not leave." His father says, "I will not leave for a while. I need to hear what you have to ask me." " Why were you so angry at me?" asks Rob.

"I never explained my actions to you," answers Rob's father. "I always wanted you to have the best life possible. I wanted you to have all the opportunities I did not have. I thought you were lazy, that you were squandering all these opportunities. It caused me distress. I did not know how to motivate you except through yelling and beating. I really did not know of any other way. And then when I got sick, I lost all sense of balance. I had these raging headaches. Sometimes they hurt so badly I could not walk. I could barely see, and I could not remember anything. Do you remember when I forgot to tell my boss I was going on vacation? Well, I was in for a big surprise when I was fired the day I returned to work.

The day you hit me, and I walked away was an overwhelming time for me. I did not understand my rage, and I certainly did not understand your response to me. Walking away seemed my one and only option. Rob, I lost the ability to express my thoughts or feelings. I was not so angry with you, not really. I was frightened of what was happening to me, and it came out as uncontrolled rage. It was not your fault that you hit me. You were only trying to protect yourself. Please stop beating up on yourself. The real tragedy is that we ran out of time to work this all out. In truth, I was dead long before I was placed in the casket. Every day was a blur for me. They said I had a stroke. Perhaps I really suffered from a brain tumor."

Rob says, "I know you are really dead, Dad. I think I know who you are. You are my father's spirit. You are the spirit I can reach when my heart is open."

His father's spirit replies; "You are right, son. I am only a spirit. I live out in the universe and I live inside you. Remember the old, disheveled guy? Well he is part of us too. Look, there he is. Son, it is time to let him go. Do you know how to do this and why it is so important?"

"Yes," answers Rob. "I have been holding on to the Mean Father by obsessing about the day I hit you. I have been holding on by blaming myself for the abuse I suffered. The holding on has brought only bitterness to my life."

The spirit says, "You are right on the mark. I want to share something you may not be aware of. Your holding on to the bitterness keeps me from my destiny. I keep floating around with no one except the mean part to accompany me. If you release me, I can finally go home."

"Where is that?" asks Rob. "That is a place where I can lay myself down and fall into a deep restful sleep," says his father's spirit. "Then what happens?" asks Rob. "Who knows?" says the spirit, "but I trust that it will be filled with adventure, pleasure and understanding."

A Grandfather and his Grandson are hugging each other tightly. They give so much love to each other. There are peaceful smiles on their faces. All is right in the world. Rob remembers when his father used to hug him. He cries. Tears roll down his face like a floodgate finally opened. He misses his father beyond words.

Shiva, The Mayan God and Goddess, the Drummer and the Warrior King all join Rob for this Releasing Ceremony. He faces his Father's Spirit and the Mean Father. The Mean Father says something. Rob asks all those present to be quiet so Rob can hear the Mean Father. He softly says, "I am sorry Rob. I am so sorry I hurt you. I am sorry that you took the blame, and I am so sorry I left you so suddenly."

Rob hugs his Mean Father and Spirit Father. He says, "I know it is time to let you go. For the first time in my life, I know what letting go actually means. It means saying goodbye." It is late in the evening. Rob lights ten candles circling the grave. He slowly raises his arms until they are over his head. As he moves his arms, he sees his the Spirit of his Father and his Mean Father fly off into the night sky. He raises his head. The two fathers merge together as one. His Father is smiling for once, "Goodbye Rob. I will always love you."

COMMENTARY
CHAPTER TWENTY-FOUR - *I NEVER SAID GOODBYE*

MAJOR CHARACTERS
Death played by The Grim Reaper
Vain Woman played by herself
The Cheetah played by himself
Fertility God and Goddess played by themselves
St. Martin De Porres played by himself
Rob's Mean Father played by himself
Rob's Father's Spirit played by himself
Grandfather and Grandson played by themselves
Shiva, Mayan God and Goddess, The Drummer and Warrior King played by themselves

I learned the meaning of letting go. I developed a ritual that involved a candle lighting ceremony, bringing in the gods and goddesses. The ceremony also included the raising of my arms and releasing my father to a place he could call home.

My father was physically and verbally abusive towards me. He also withdrew from me, which perhaps was the most painful wound. I trust that his spirit was communicating the truth. I believed that those were his words, not some fantasy of mine.

I learned how bitterness forms and what role it played in my life. Bitterness is exaggerated numbness. I learned that bitterness blocks access to the heart.

The entry of the gods and goddesses and the eternal truths they represent helped me to release my bitterness toward my father. I realized that he and I were both doing the best we could in difficult situations, in a tiny part of the infinite cycle of life and death. Seeing that truth enabled me to let him go to his destiny, and freed me to seek my own.

FAMILY DISCUSSION QUESTIONS
For Chapter Twenty-Four - *I NEVER SAID GOOD-BYE*

1.   Rob realizes that he never said good-bye to his father before he died. Have you ever had a similar experience?

2.   Rob hits his father in the stomach during this chapter. How do you feel about this?

3.   Rob's father does not retaliate against Rob, and he dies shortly after this altercation. How do you feel about this?

4.   Rob talks about a black cloud hanging over his head. Have you ever felt this way?

5.   Rob experiences bitterness in this chapter. Have you ever felt bitter?

6.   Rob talks about his father's beatings. Have you ever been physically or verbally abused?

7.   How do you feel about the ending of this book?

ACKNOWLEDGEMENTS

I give thanks to: Gisela Schubach De Domenico for sharing her teaching, wisdom support, and encouragement. David Spero for his editing, friendship-always being there and honesty. The C sisters-I hope happiness will find you someday. Rosa and her wonderful family who proved that miracles do happen. The S/B family who taught us how to face incredible adversity. Susan Solomon who created the wonderful cover illustration. My mother for her love, patience and willingness to step into my shoes. My sister for her commitment to build a new relationship with me. All my friends who have been there for me while I have been immersed in this work. My wife, Gail Meadows for being my best friend all these years. When the sun is behind you and your brown eyes radiate on my soul, I know that the best times are now.

ADDITIONAL CREDITS

Cover Illustrations
Susan Solomon SFClan@aol.com

Sandtray photos Onc through Fifteen
Gail Meadows and Nebiet Barham

Sandtray Photos Sixteen through Twenty-Four
Gisela Schubach De Domenico, Ph.D

ABOUT THE AUTHOR

Bob Livingstone was born in Boston and raised in Highland Park, New Jersey. This is his first book, and he hopes to write others. He has survived his father's death, sadistic teachers, inept coaches, drug abuse, teenage self-loathing, and several years in the state of Kansas.

He is a licensed clinical social worker and psychotherapist who has been in private practice since 1987. He earned a Masters Degree in Social Welfare from The University of Kansas in 1979. He works with adults, adolescents and children. He specializes in divorce, trauma, grief, teenager-parent relationships, couples counseling, and family therapy. Bob's favorite mode of treatment is Sandtray Therapy.

Redemption of the Shattered has been in the making since June 1991, and Bob is elated that it is now available for the rest of the world to read. He has reached out to his friends to participate in this endeavor, and they have provided much of the technical and creative support that has made this book what it is. Other friends and allies have assisted in the public presentation of this work. The presentation becomes a performance with shared reading, drumming and displaying of sandtray slides. The author hopes that this circle of family and friends will grow as *Redemption* is discovered.

Bob is in his early fifties and lives in San Francisco with his wife Gail. They will soon celebrate their thirtieth wedding anniversary. Please check out his web page at www.boblivingstone.com for more information on Sandtray Therapy, Bob's clinical practice, or presentations of *Redemption*.

Bob's office in the San Francisco Bay Area is located at 205 E. 3rd Ave. Suite 207, San Mateo, CA 94401. His phone number is 650-347-5167 E-mail: bobl@netwizards.net

Printed in the United States
3945